VERTICAL HORIZON

Gazing up at the Hong Kong heights

香港印象

仰望都市新角度

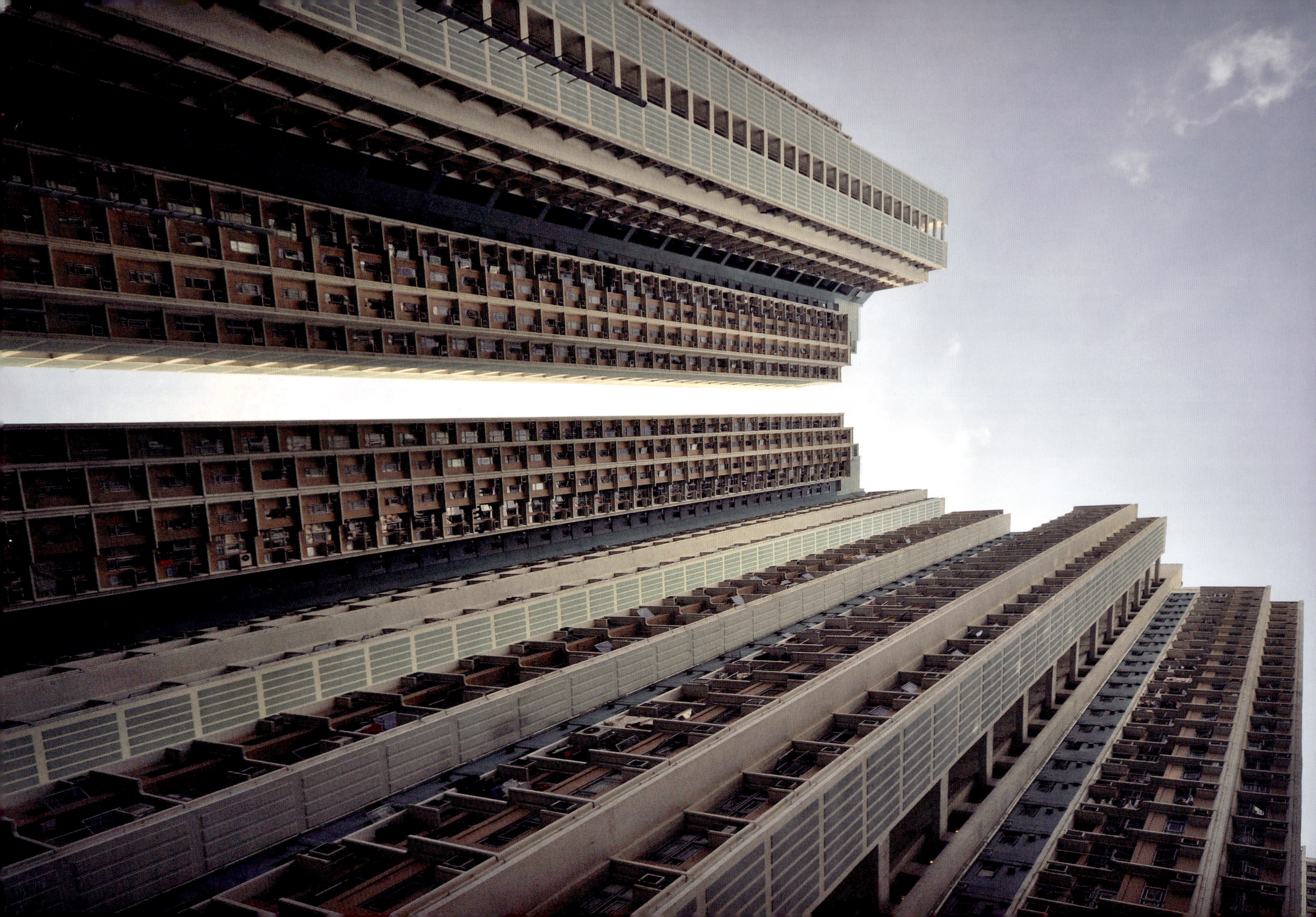

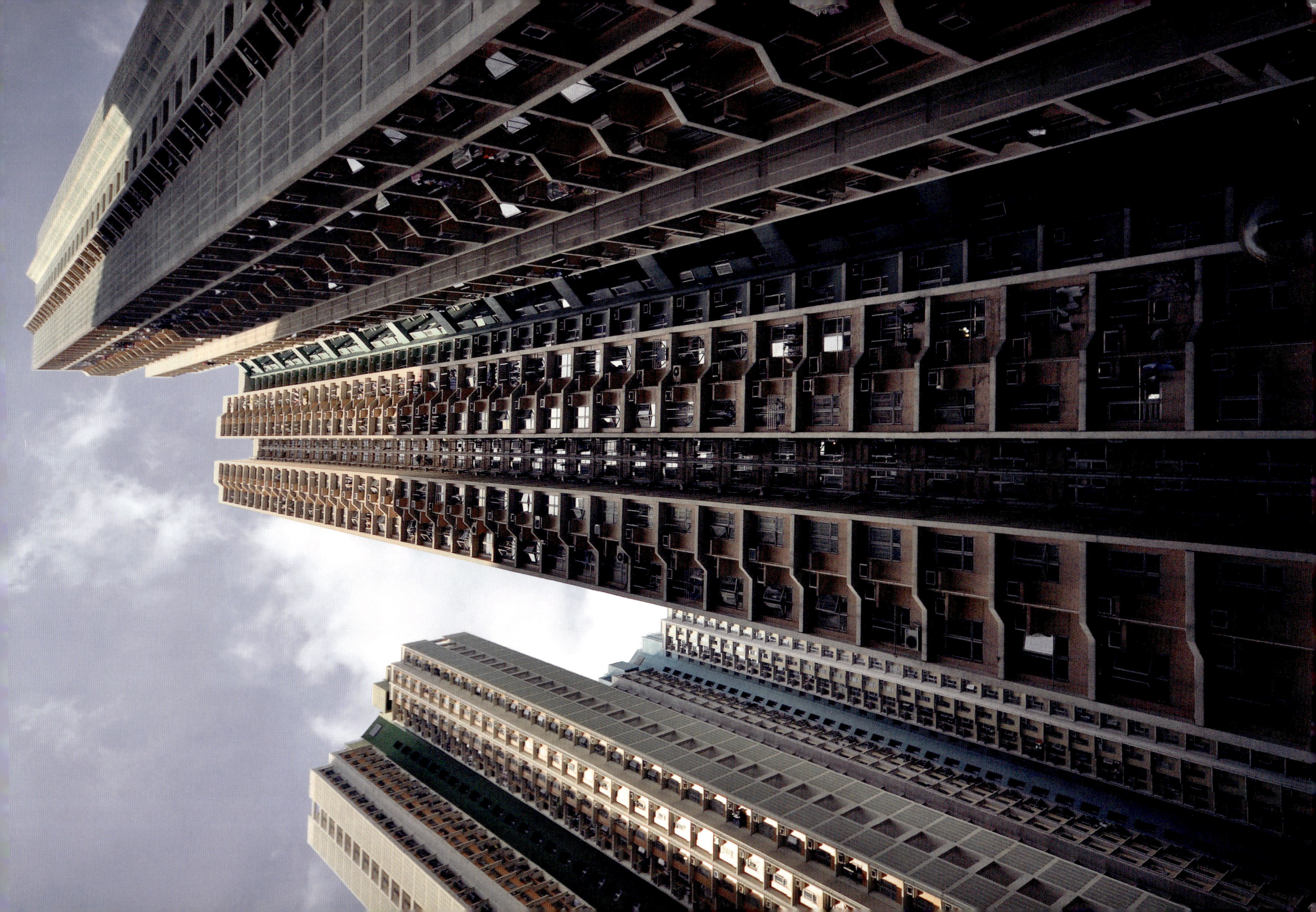

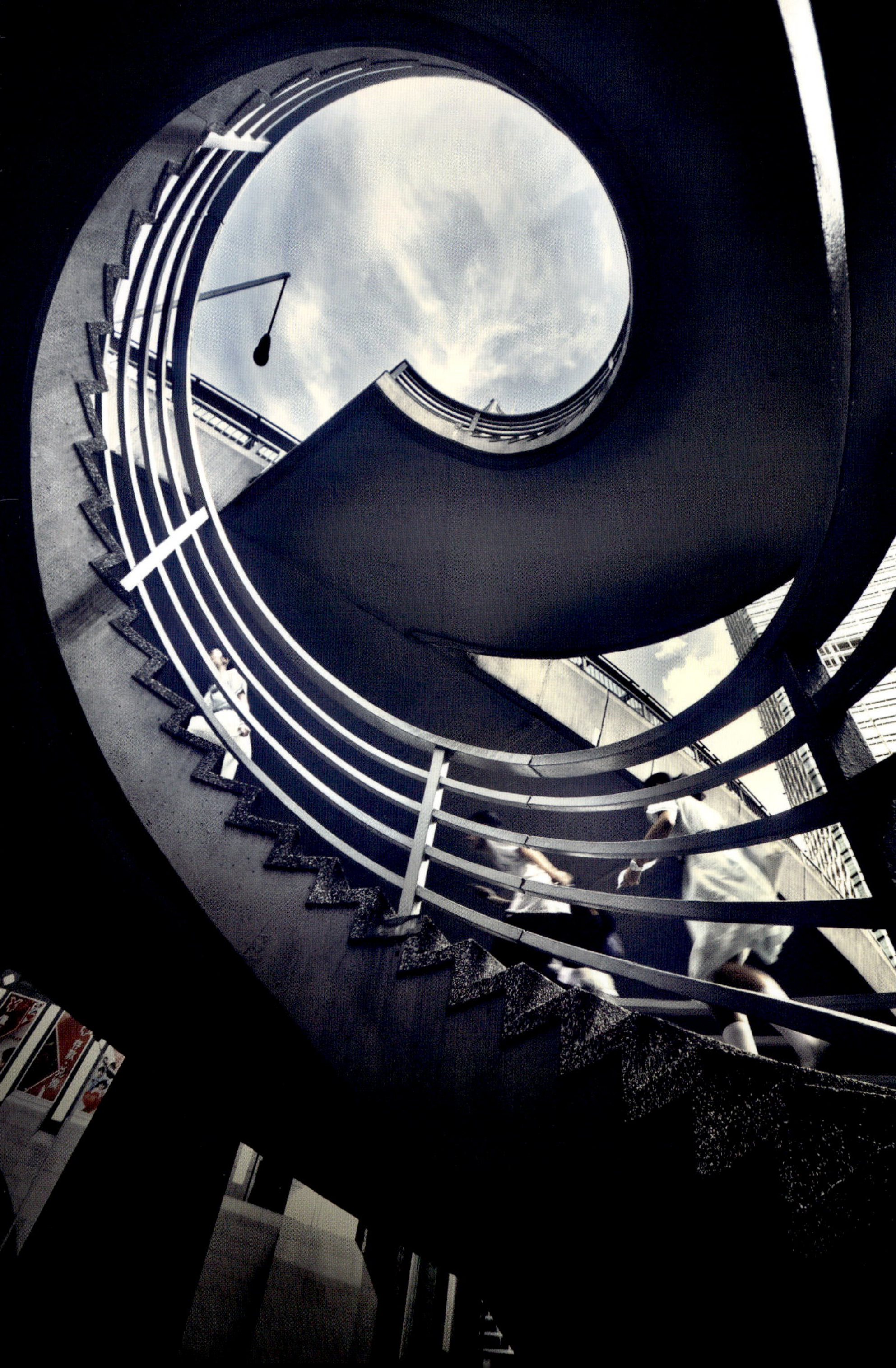

Introduction

What immediately struck me upon arriving in Hong Kong was the strong visual qualities of its buildings, and especially the traditional *tong lau* (唐樓) still found in older districts. After settling myself in Yau Tsim Mong, I was able to thoroughly explore its dense environs and diverse architecture.

I was particularly fascinated by how such a variety of buildings could blend together. Each differed to some extent – sometimes drastically – from its neighbour in size, shape, age, style and colour, and yet by being packed so closely next to another, their mix of modern and traditional contrived to look almost seamless. Some of these compact blocks were bisected by streets or cut through by ominous-looking alleys. These in turn often revealed themselves to be 'spaces out of time', bypassed by the roar of busy streets and offering both oases of calm and an arresting perspective on the buildings.

Little by little, by moving away from the heart of Kowloon, I discovered more about the Hong Kong urban environment. First, there were the business districts, seemingly composed entirely of sharp-edged skyscrapers with shimmering glass facades. While walking between them, one can appreciate interesting lighting effects as well as impressive lines of perspective.

Then I began to make forays into the New Territories' high-density residential areas and their forests of 30 to 40-storey buildings. In spite of the relatively large spaces between blocks, one can still get the impression of being surrounded by looming giants while walking among them.

Even though all these different areas seem utterly unlike each other, I eventually perceived that they did share something in common. As I lifted my head upwards searching for a scrap of sky between the buildings, the feeling of awe was always the same. To me, this impetus to strain upwards for the sky is the coherent element of Hong Kong's urban environment. I call it the 'vertical horizon'.

By following this trail, I wanted to capture the diversity of Hong Kong's urban areas, their great visual richness, and their strange unity. In making this book, I have stared at and pondered a city which fascinates me – and now I share the experience with you.

簡介

最初來到香港的時候，最讓我感到震撼的是各式摩天大廈帶來的視覺衝擊，而我更意想不到在舊區仍可發現舊式唐樓的蹤影。我一直居住在油尖旺區一帶，也許是這個高密度的市中心，促使我深入探索周邊交錯的建築群。

鬧市中，摩登樓房與破舊樓群互相毗鄰，表面上看似格格不入，但仔細觀察才發現彼此交織了一片高低起伏、形態萬千、顏色豐富的迷人景致。鱗次櫛比的建築物之間有五光十色的繁忙大街，也有陰暗寂靜的骯髒後巷。不過，就只有這些毫不起眼的小巷才可遠離繁囂，成爲寧靜而有趣的觀察點。

當我踏出九龍的中心地帶，便漸漸發現更多香港市區的面貌。港島商業區的摩天大廈高聳而立，玻璃幕牆在日光下反射多重光線，耀眼奪目。要是在高樓大廈之間穿梭仰望，這些特別效果就更爲壯觀。

新界區的景象則截然不同，映入眼簾的滿是一群群三、四十層高的新建高密度住宅，猶如森林一樣。雖然這裡的樓宇之間空間較大，但置身其中，仍彷彿給巨塔重重包圍。

香港每個地區的建築物也有其微妙的共通之處。每當我仰望高樓之間的一片天空，總不禁嘖嘖稱奇。不斷往高空發展的建築物，其實也一直在垂直的地平線上延伸，希望連接天際。

這城市確實令我著迷，透過《香港印象》，我希望以嶄新角度充分展現香港最真實的城市面貌，並分享這個城市最多元、豐富的視覺體驗。

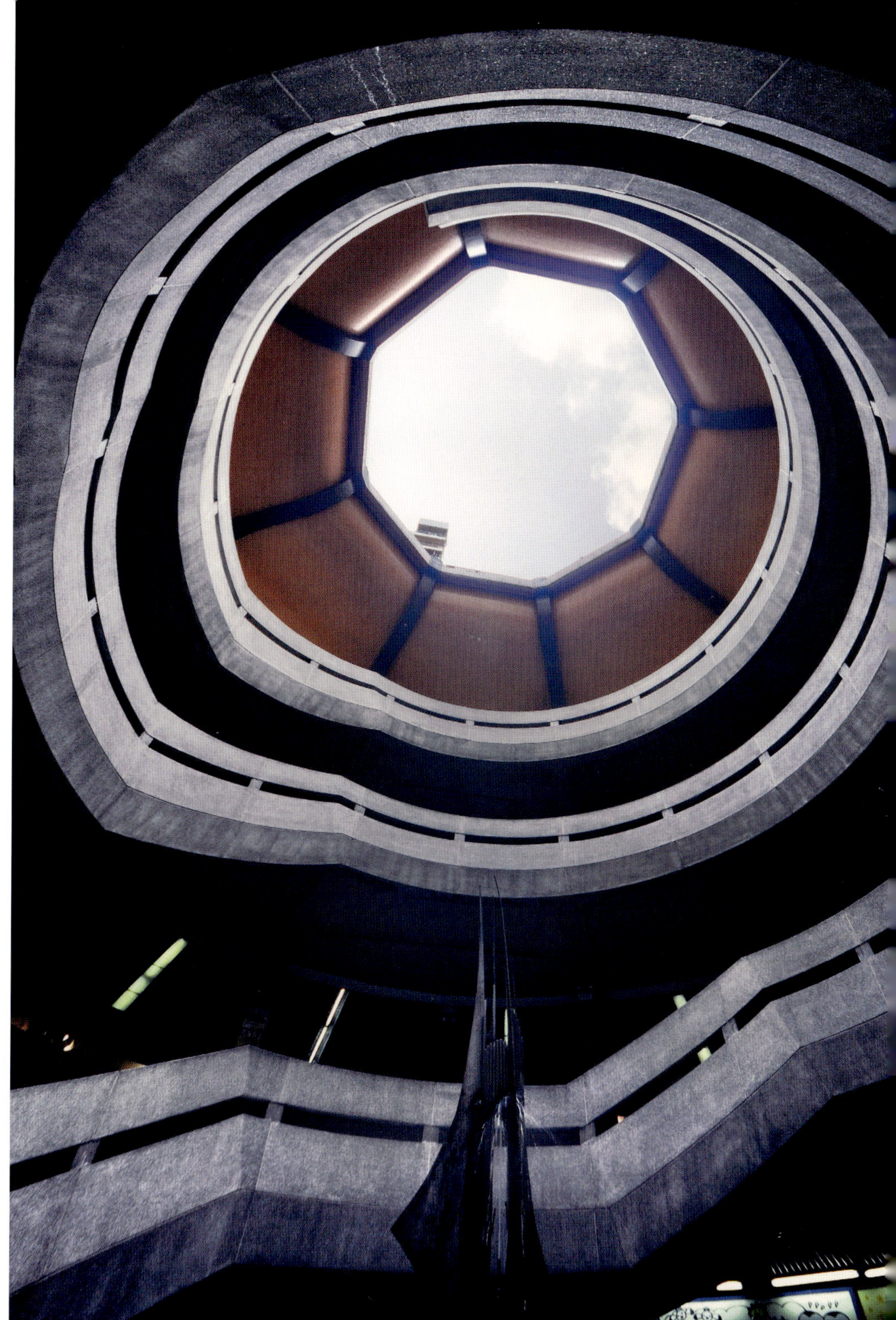

穿透

Penetrating

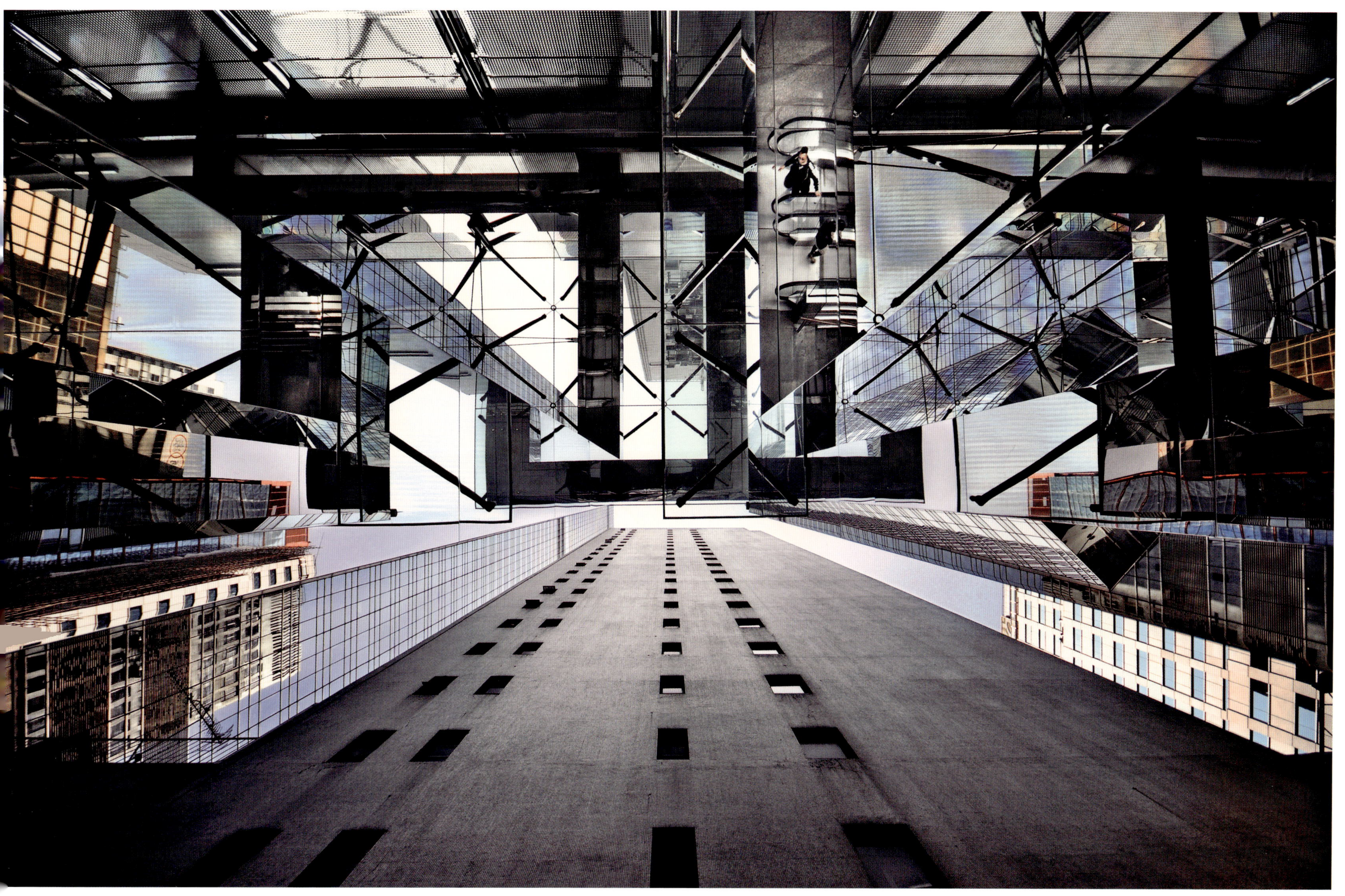

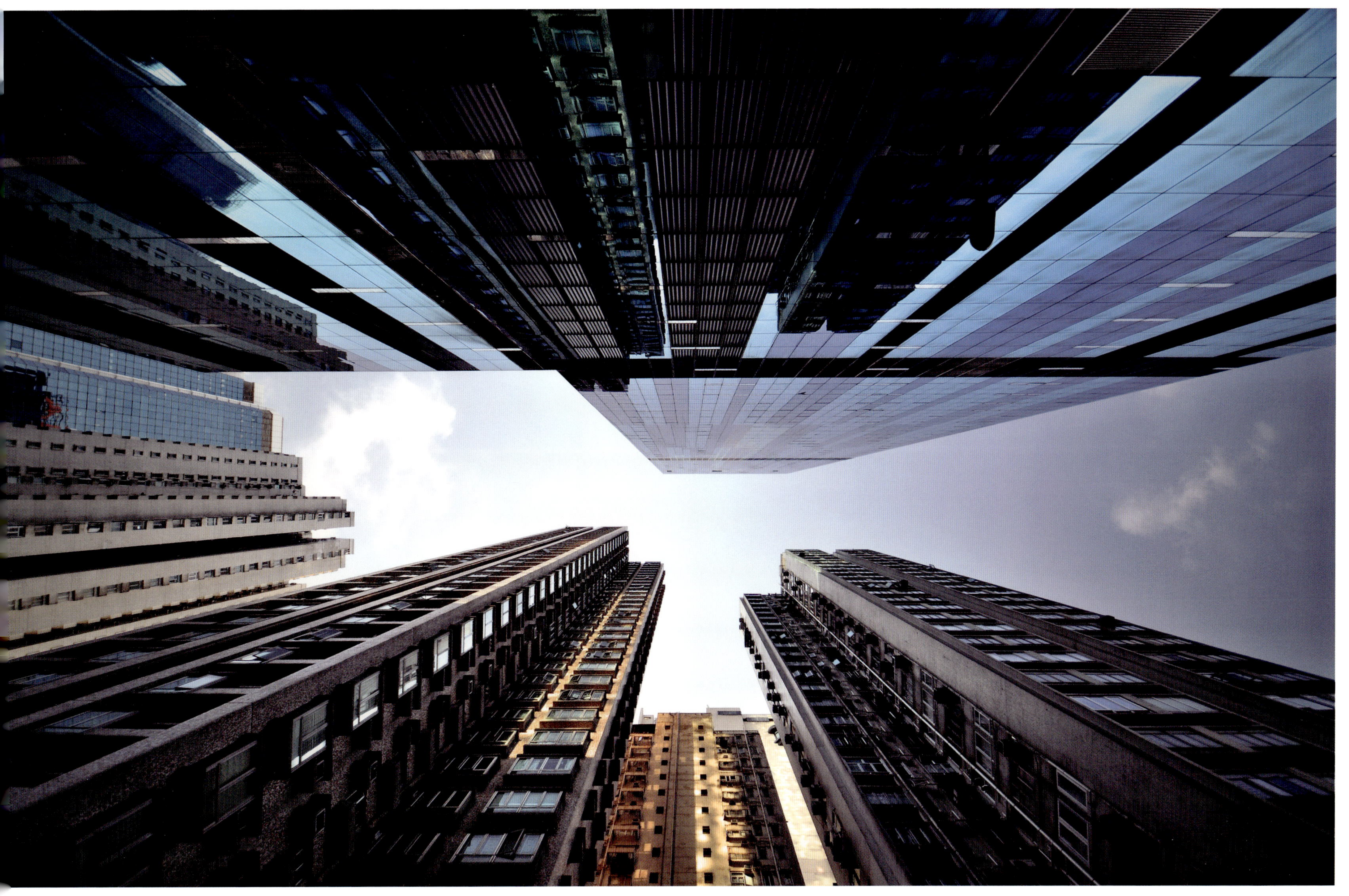

鋒芒

Trenchant Swords

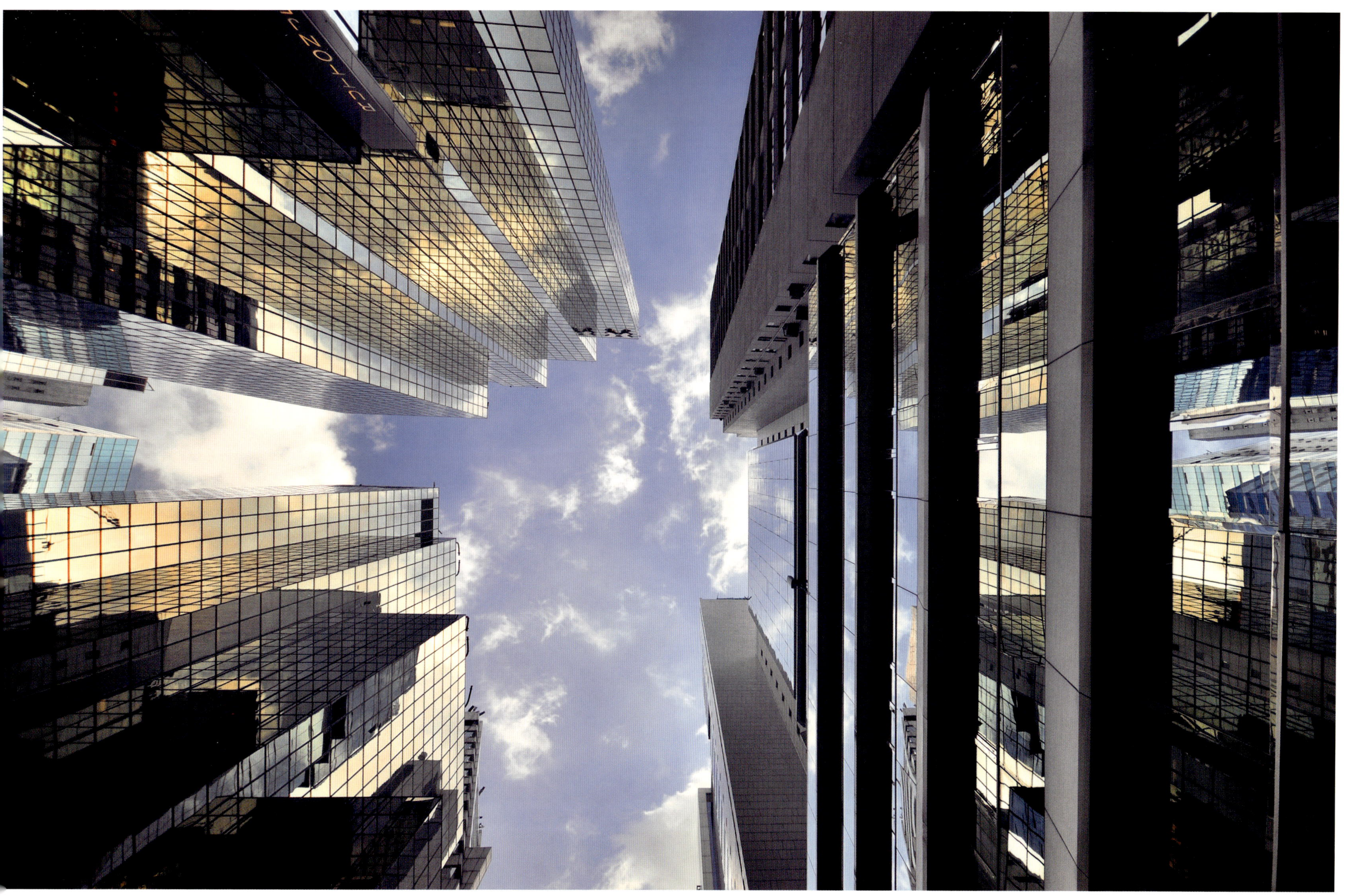

棱鏡

Prism

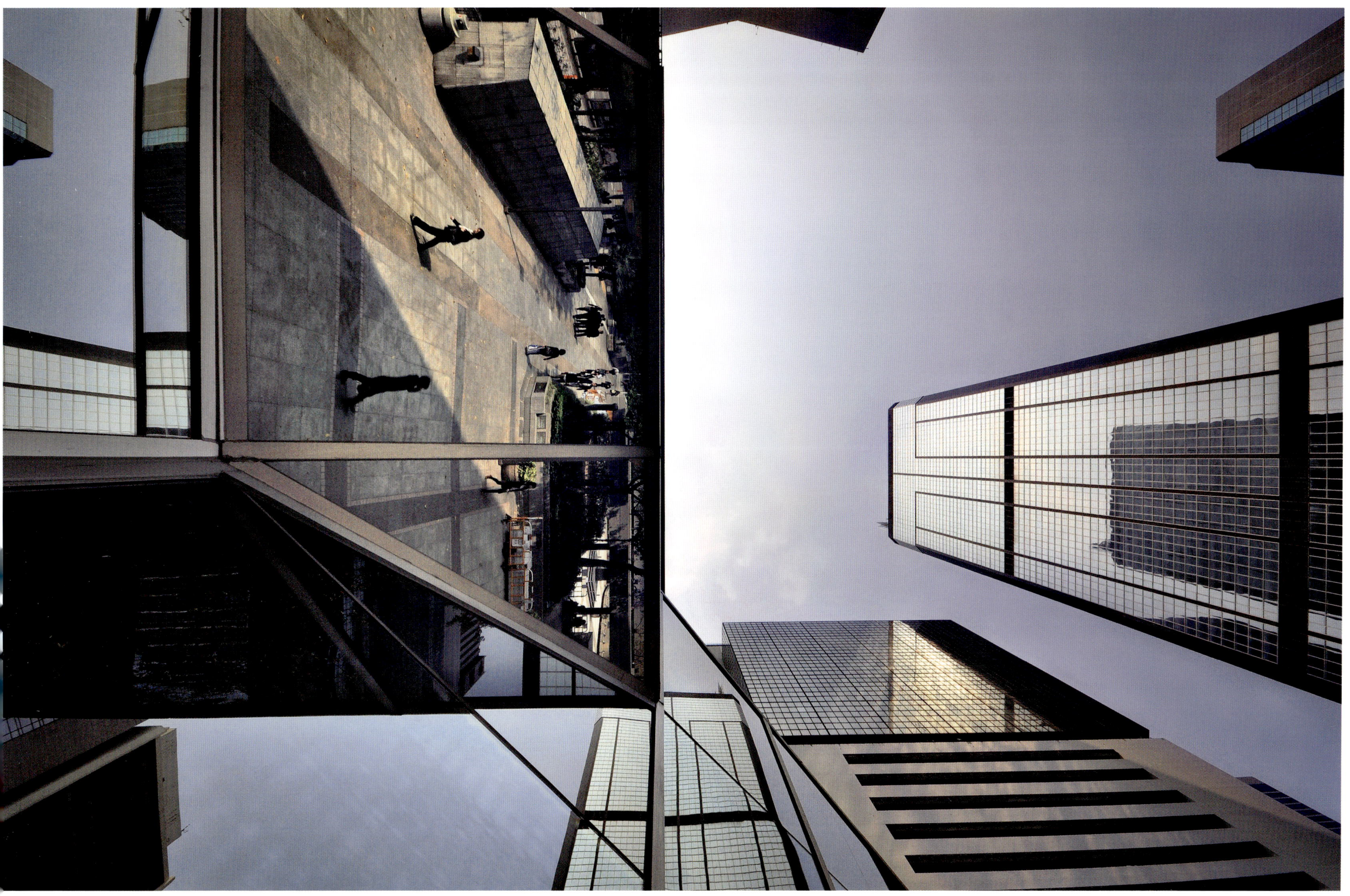

速度

Speed

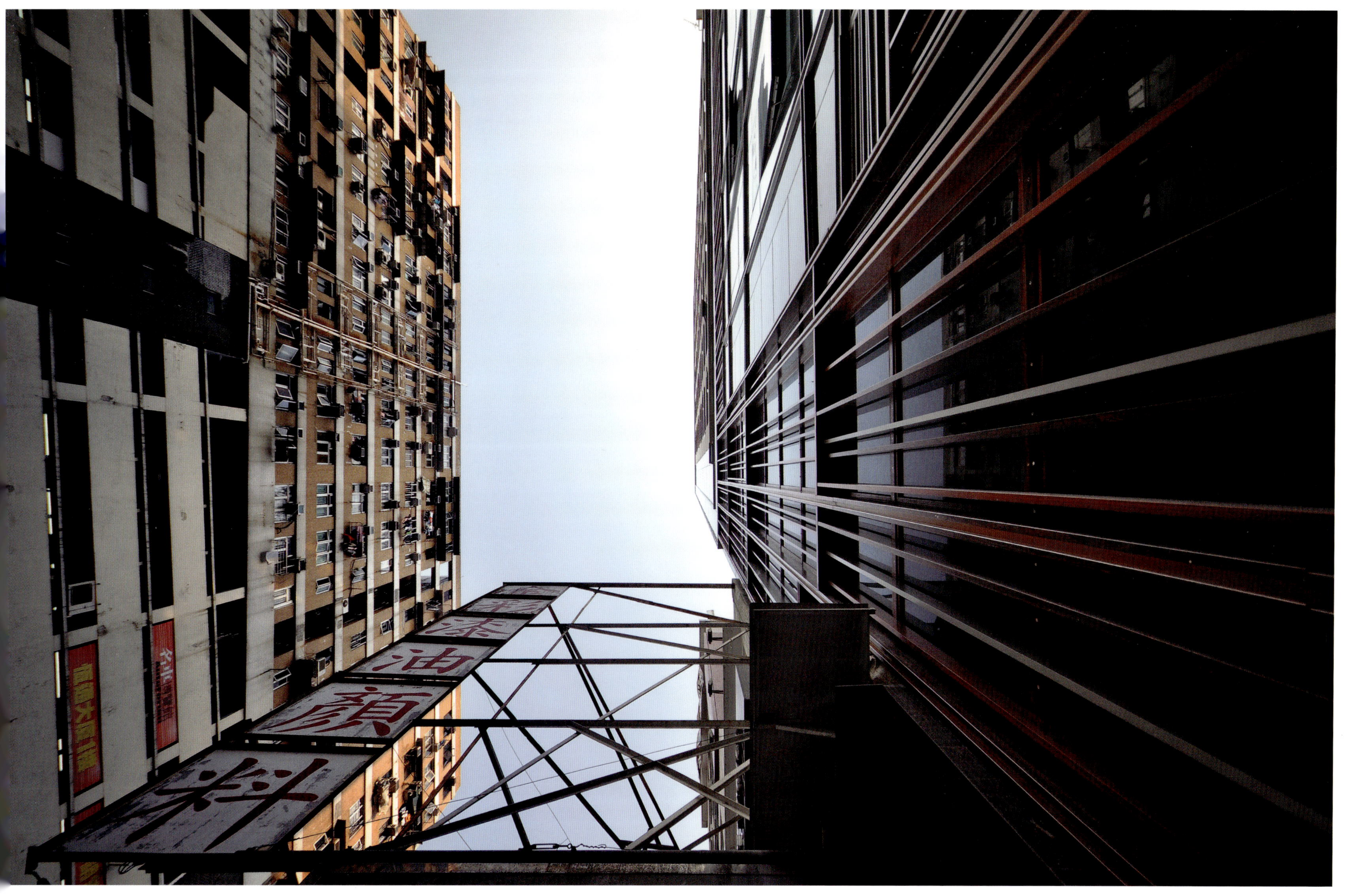
漆
油
顏
料

同天空

Shared Sky

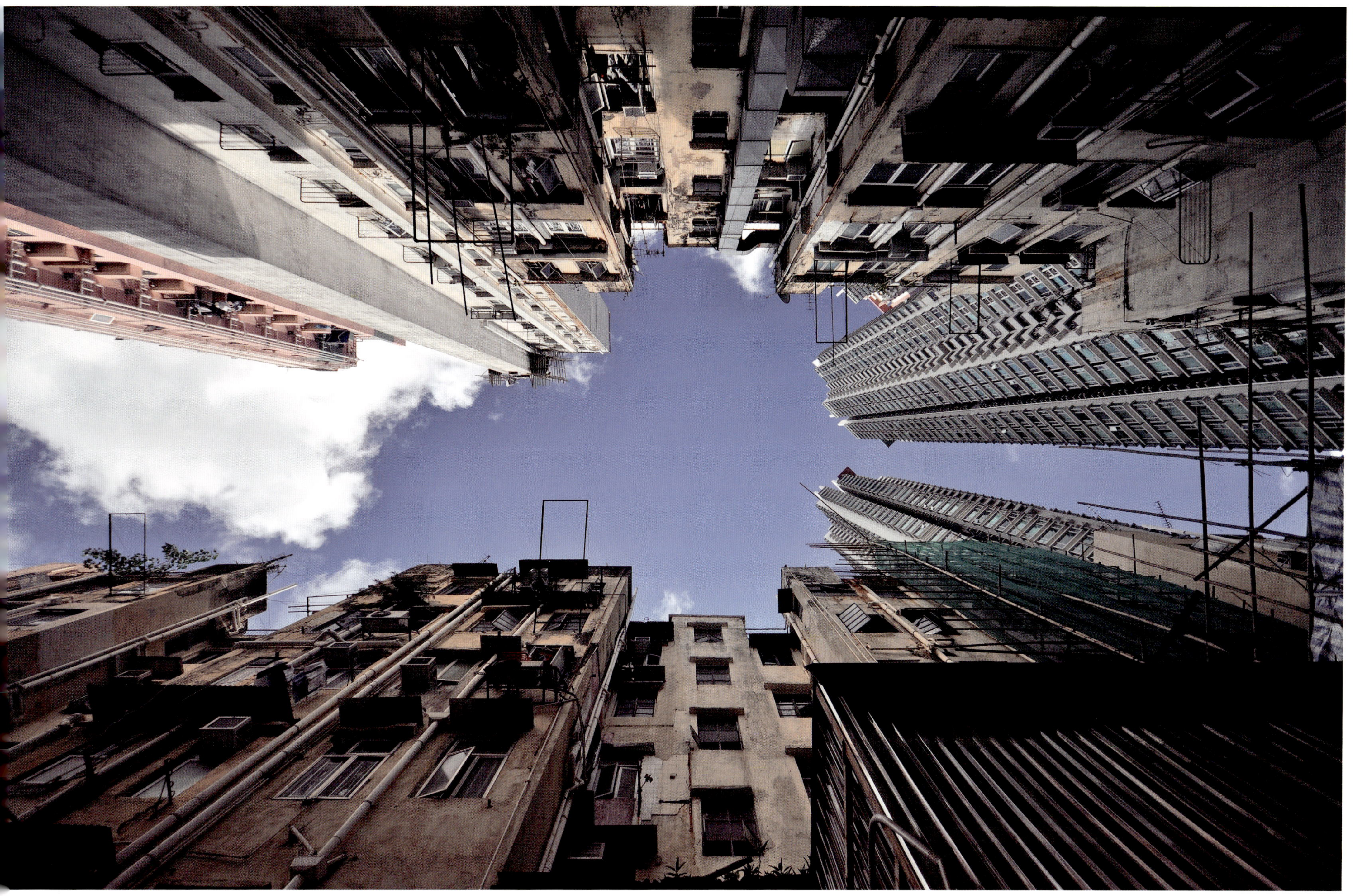

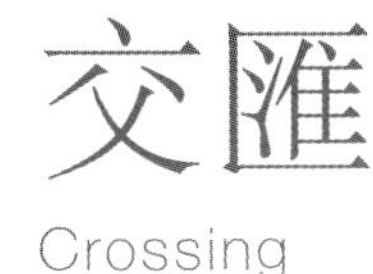

交匯

Crossing

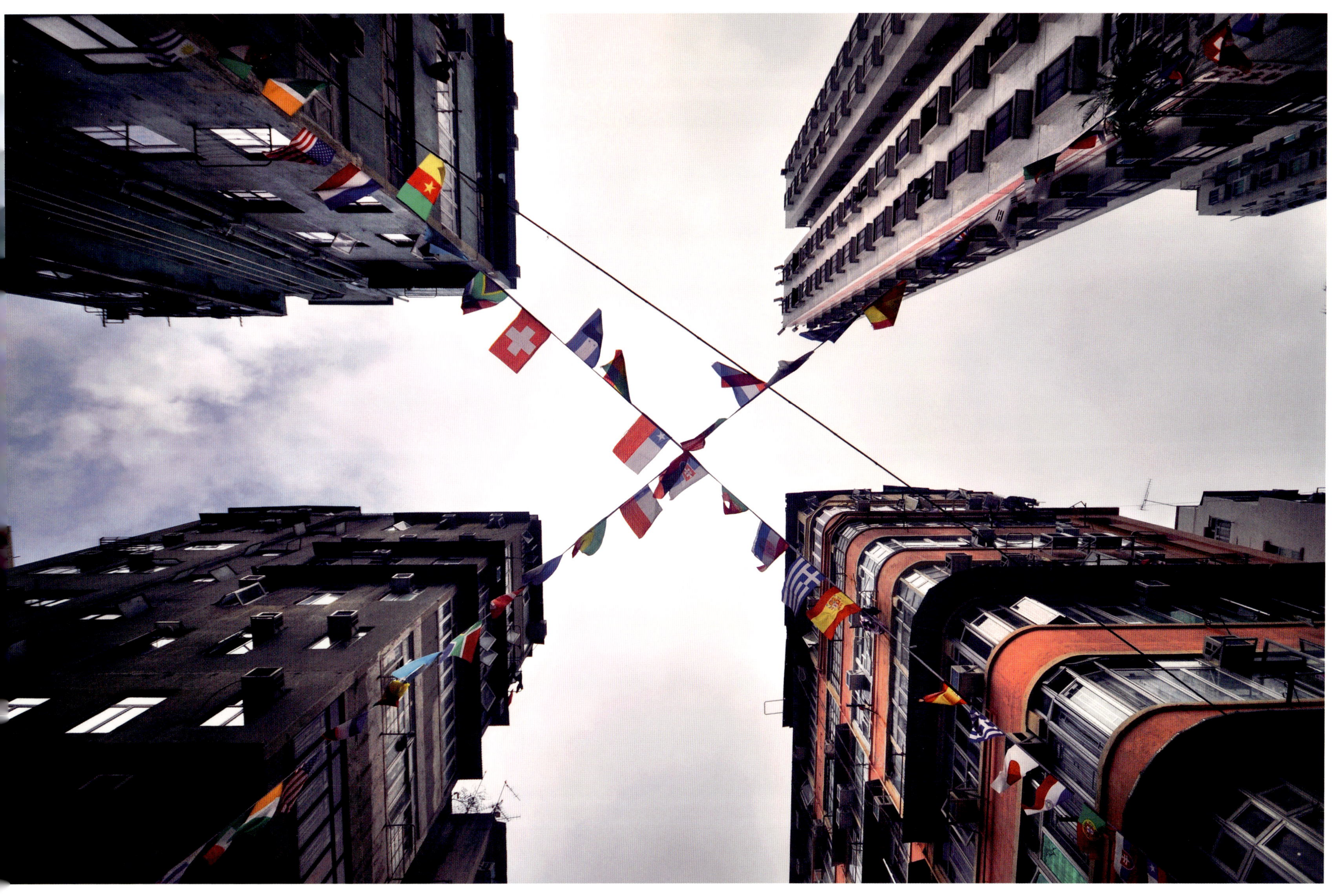

朱紅

Vermilion

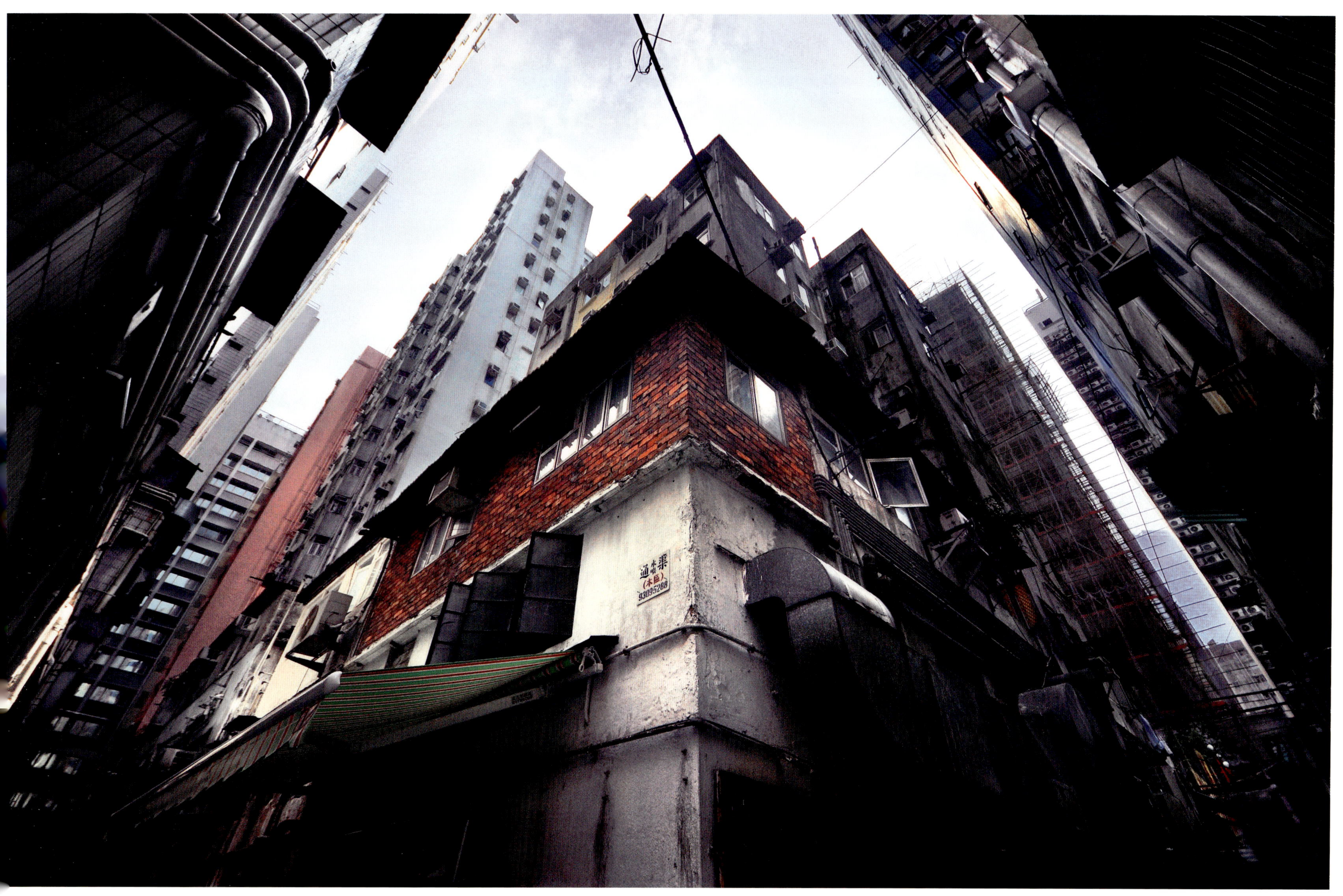

通渠
水喉
(本區)
93095288

拼字遊戲

Scrabble

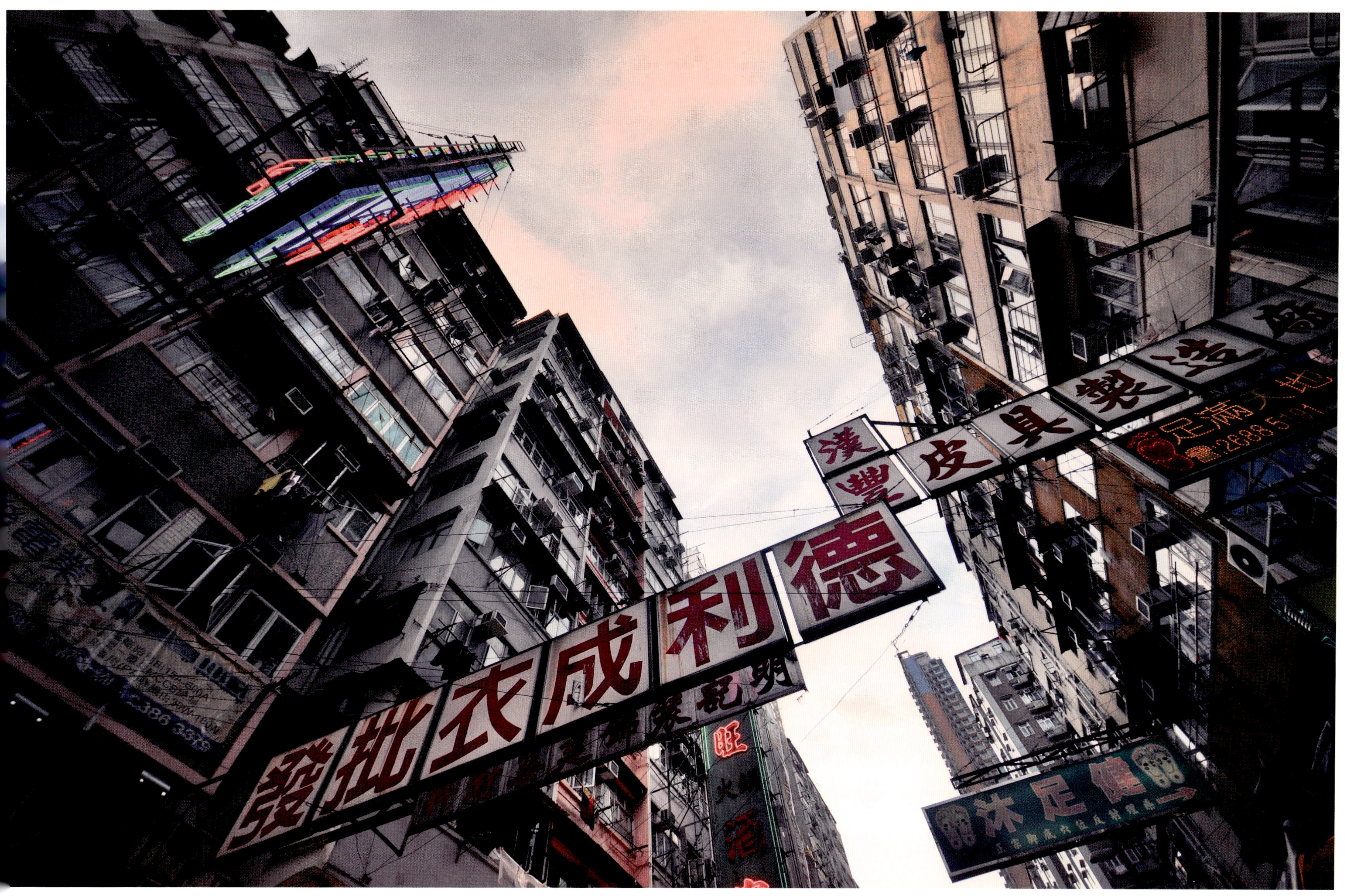

德利成衣批發
漢豐
皮具製
2688 5101
健足沐
旺

居高臨下

Overlook

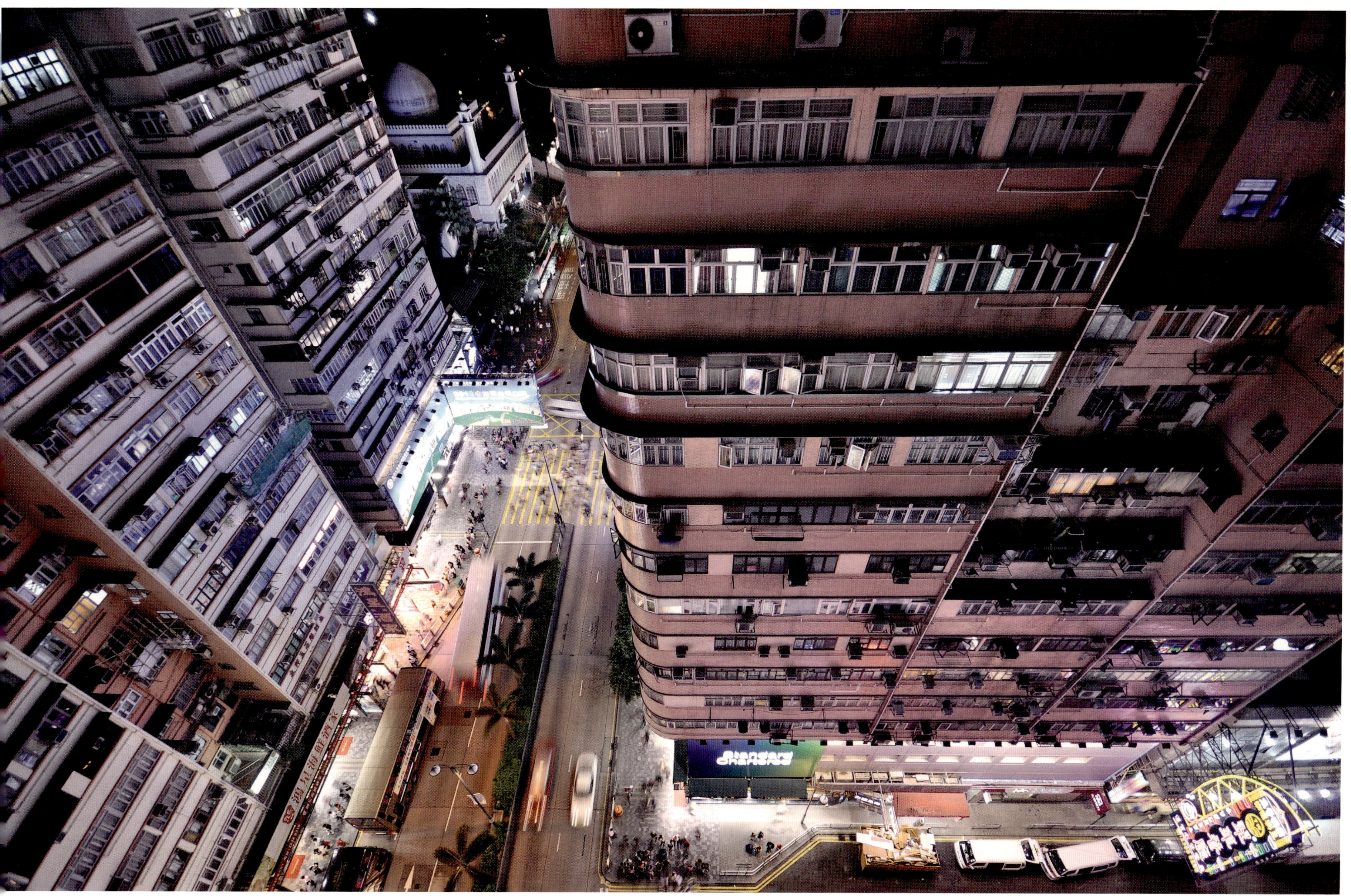
Standard Chartered

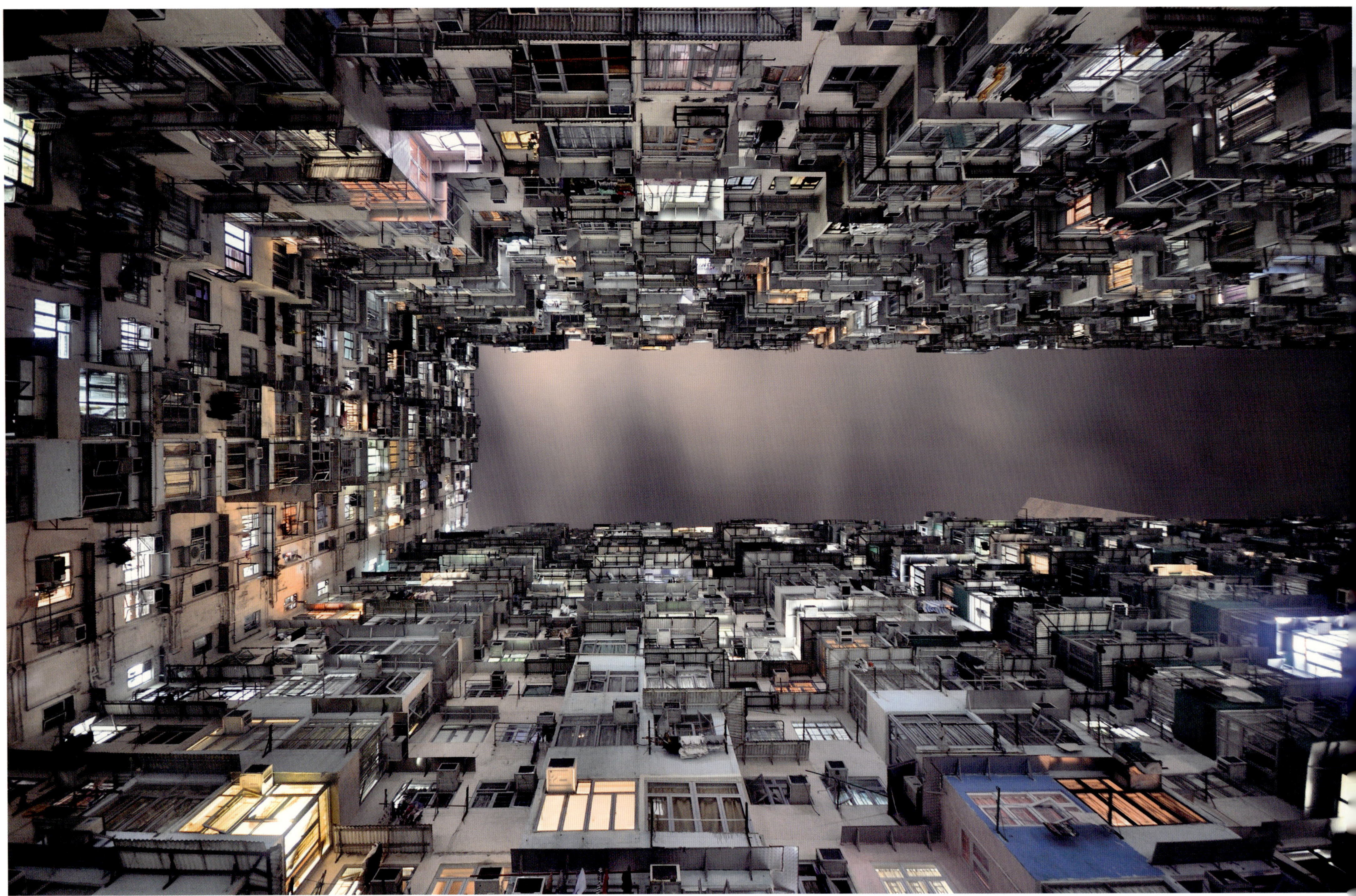

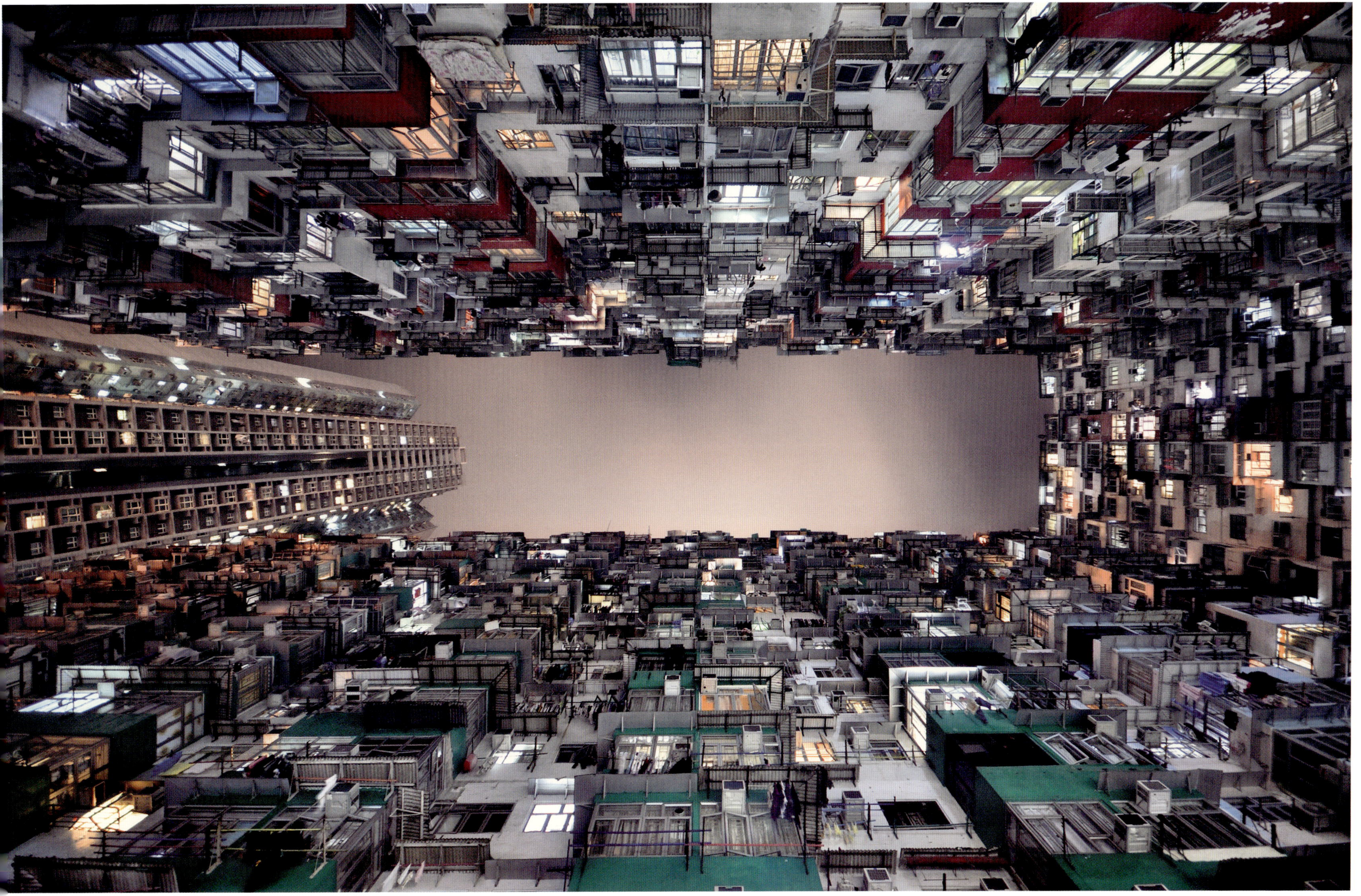

延伸

Reach

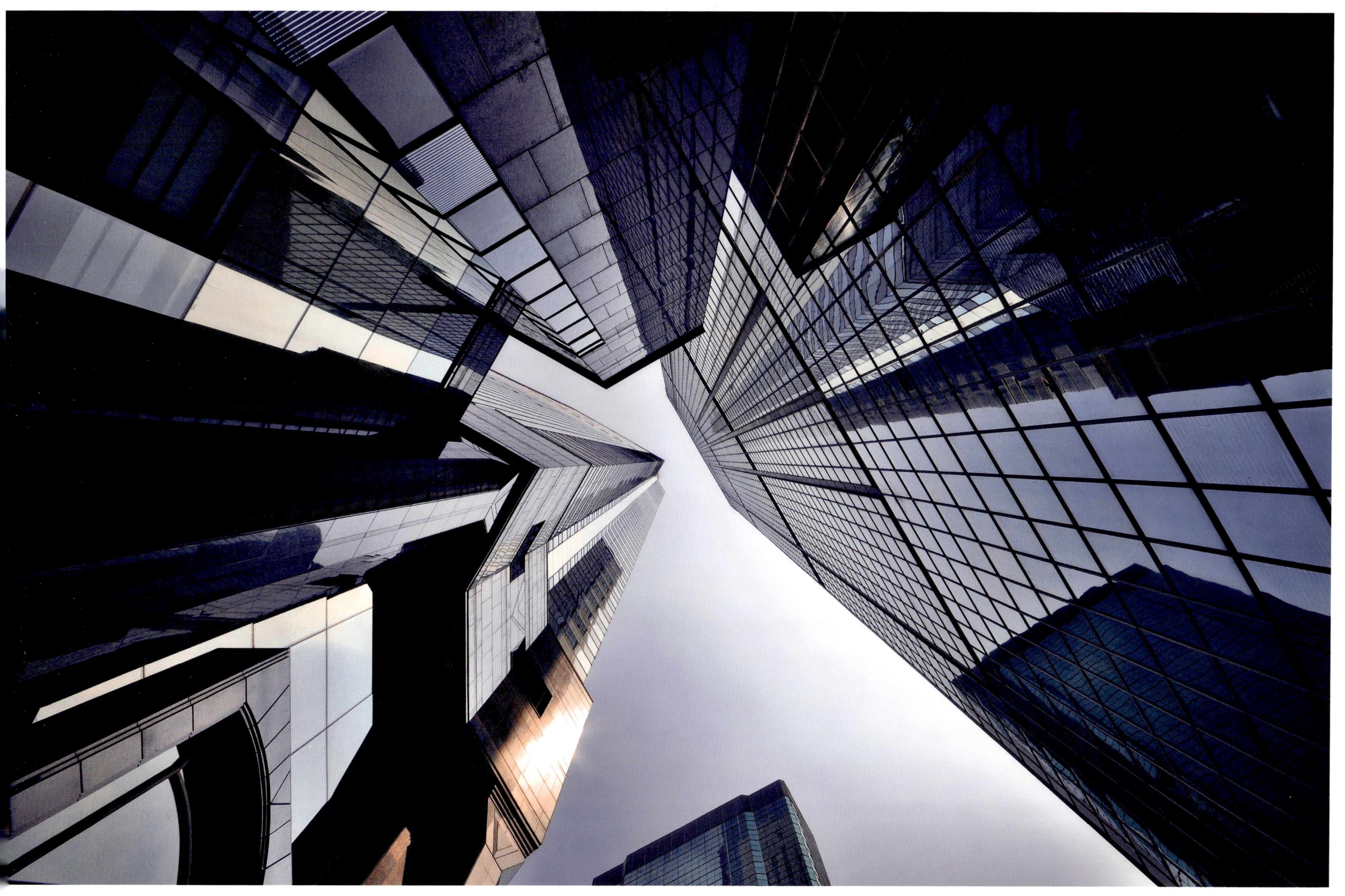

玻璃之城

City of Glass

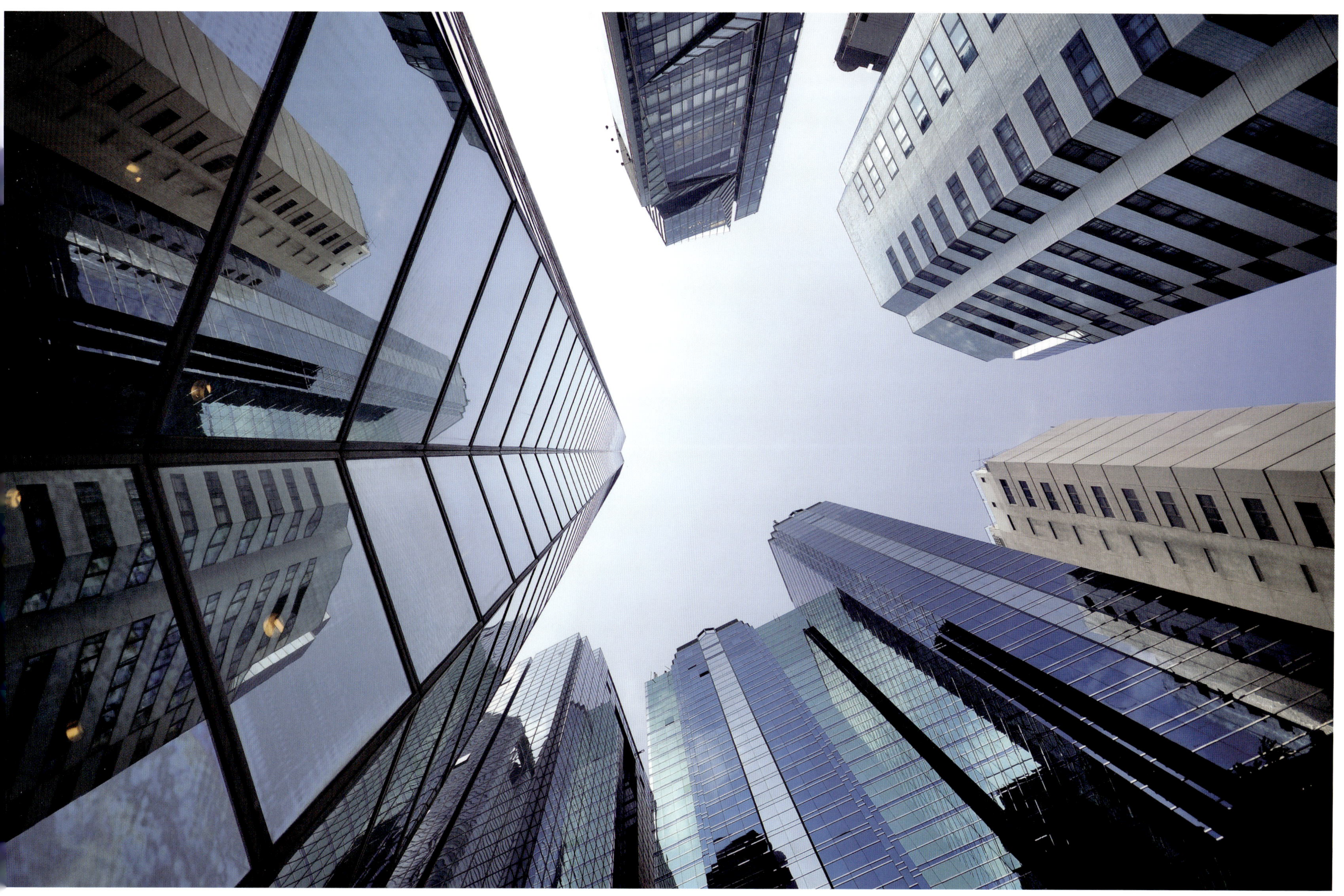

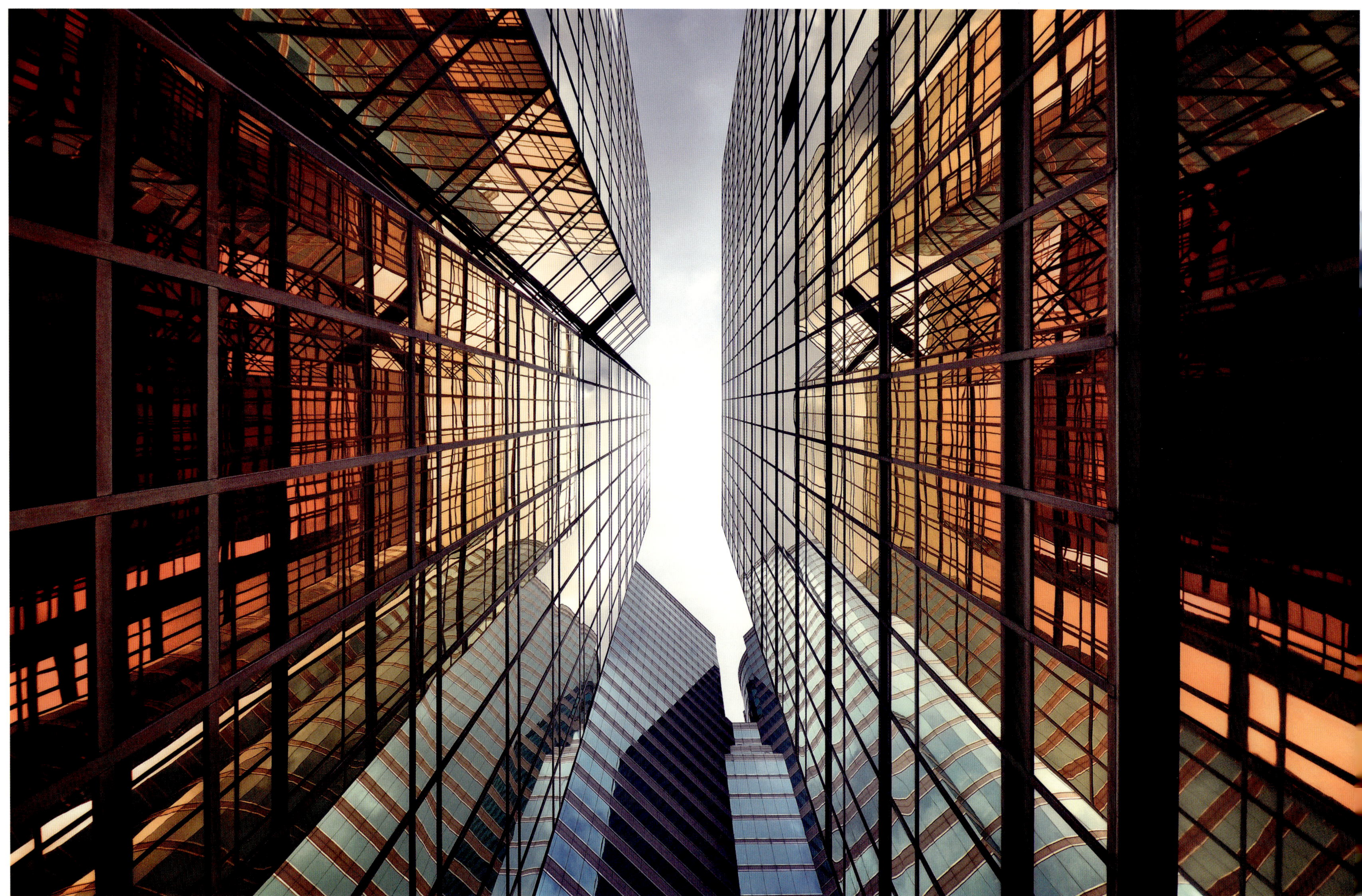

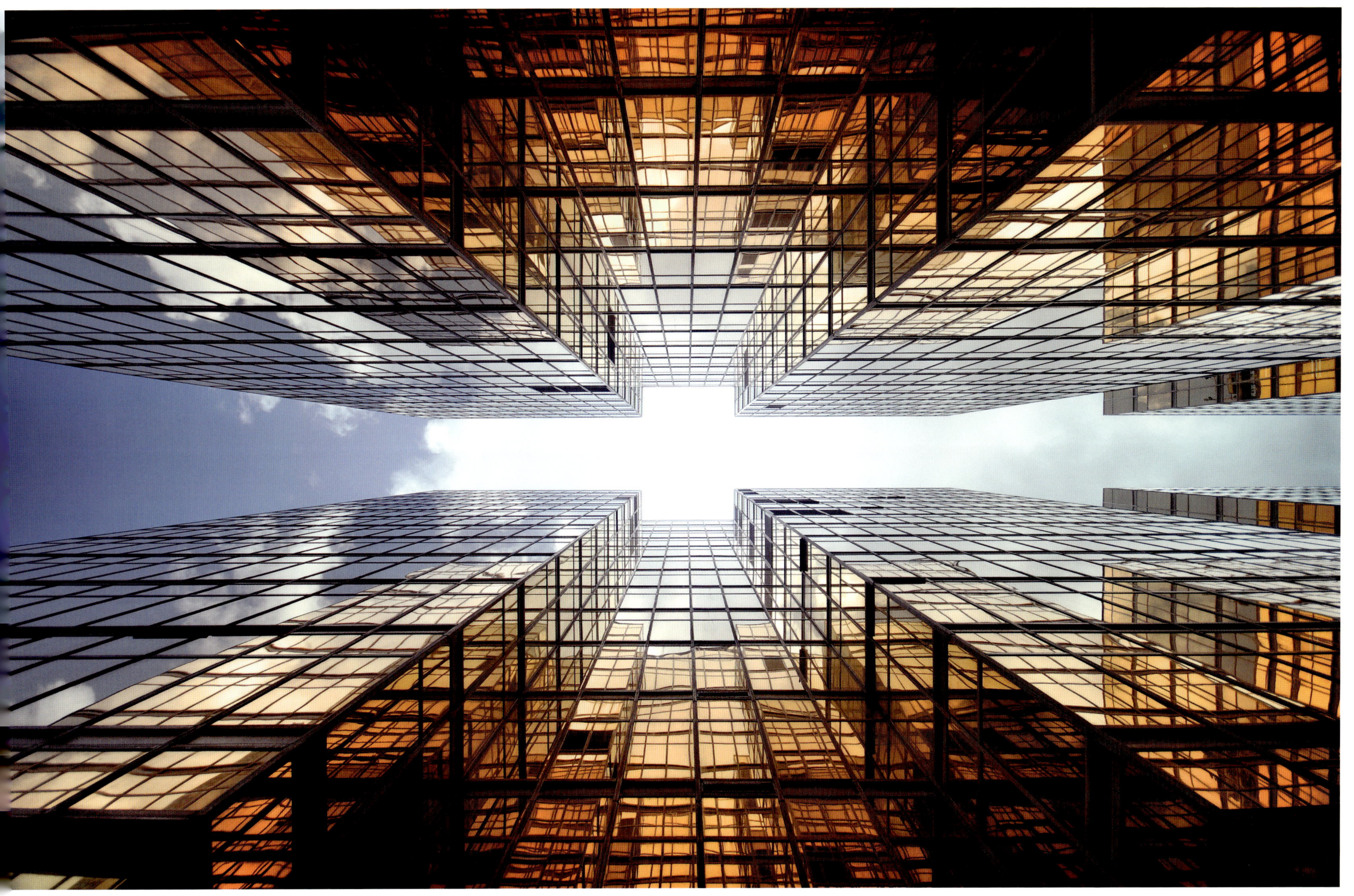

黃金時代
Golden Age

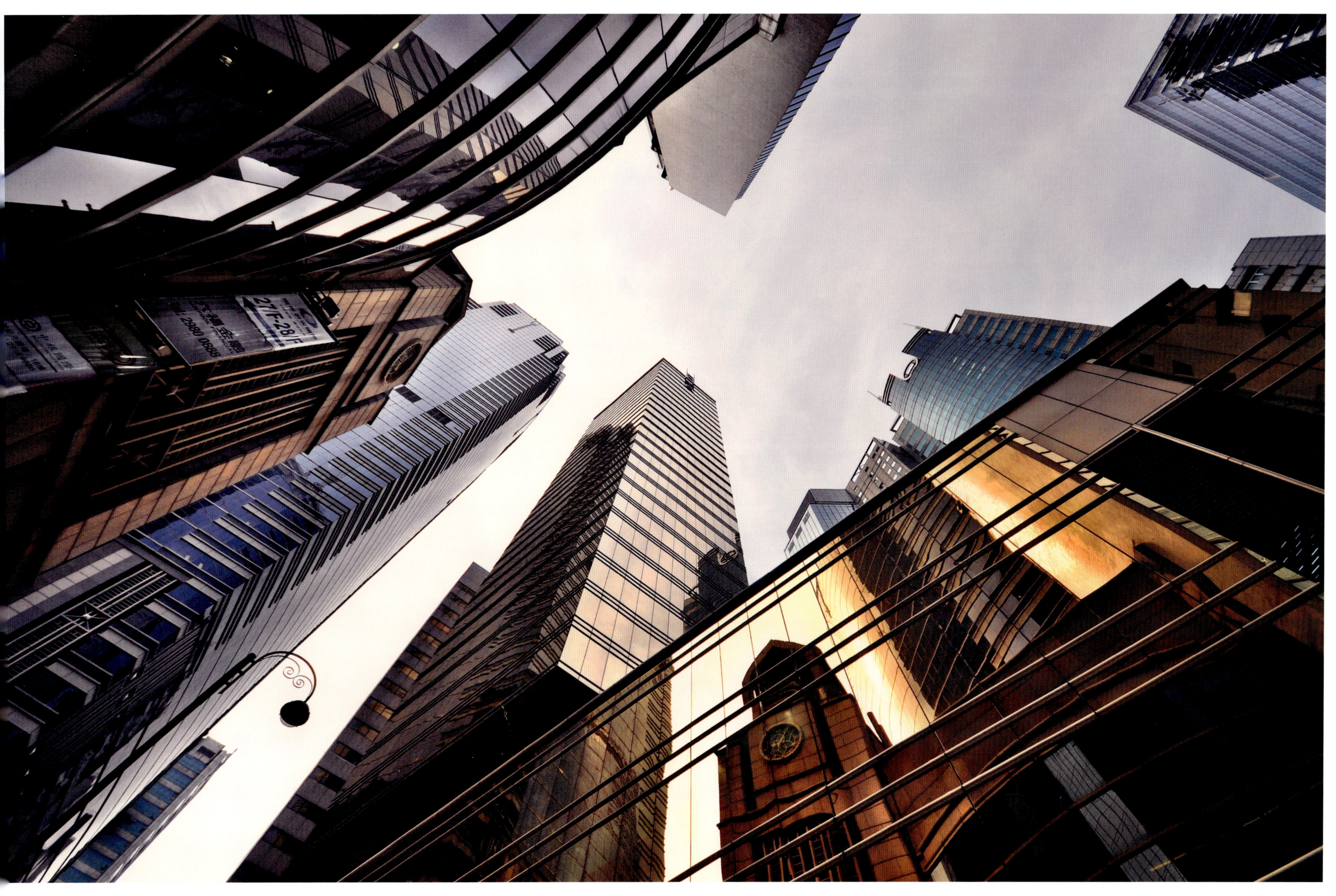
27/F-28/F
2980 0888

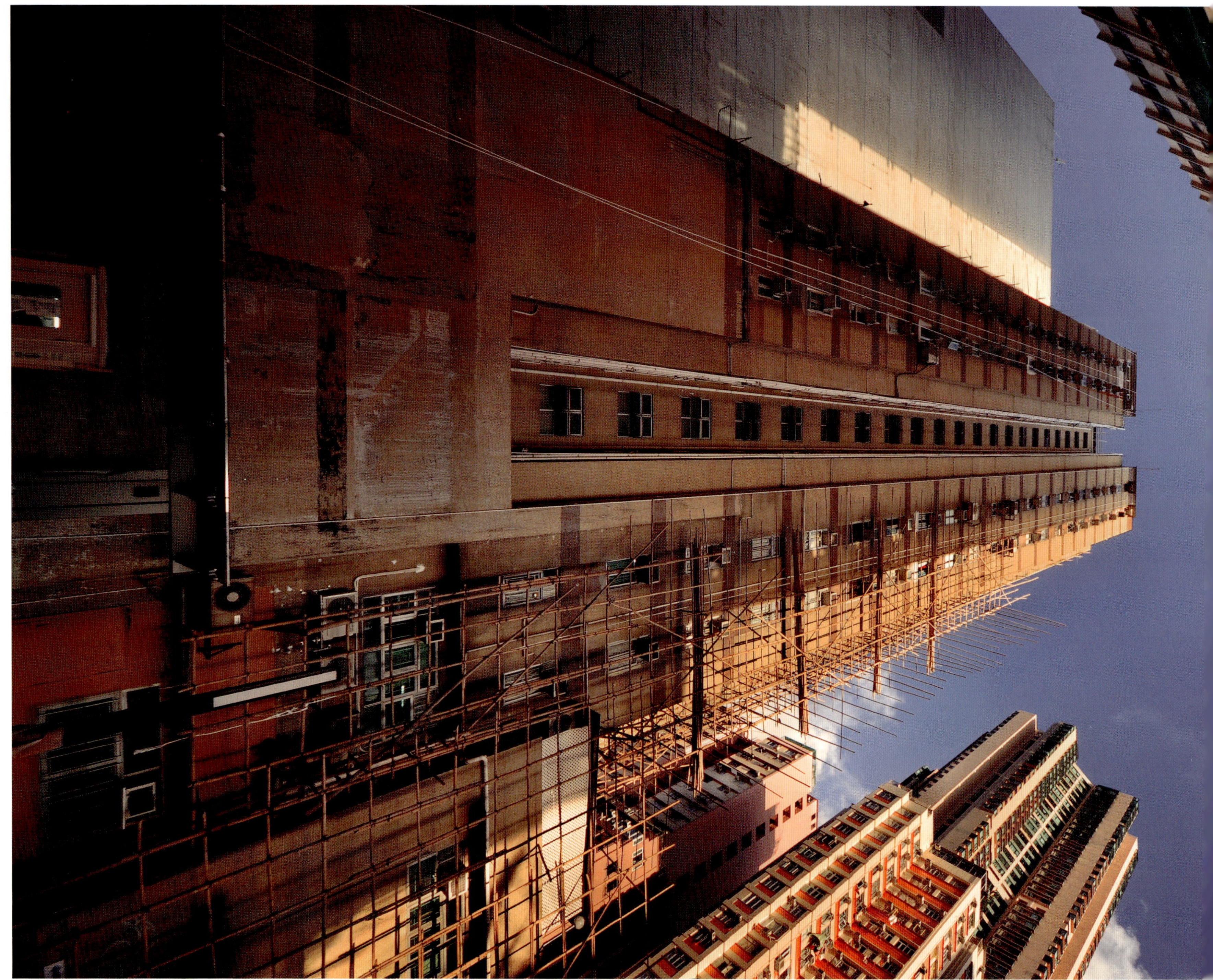

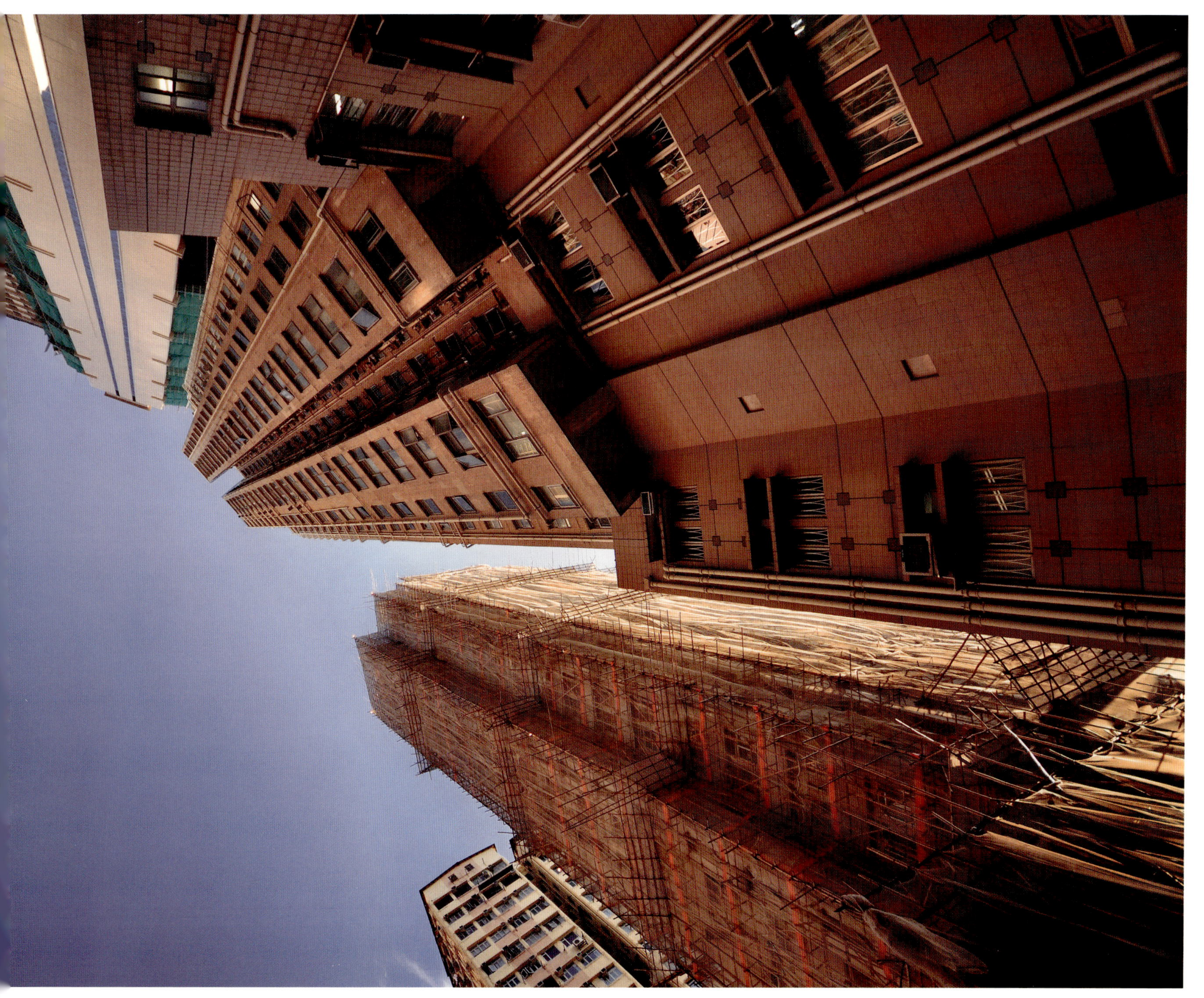

攀緣

Climbers

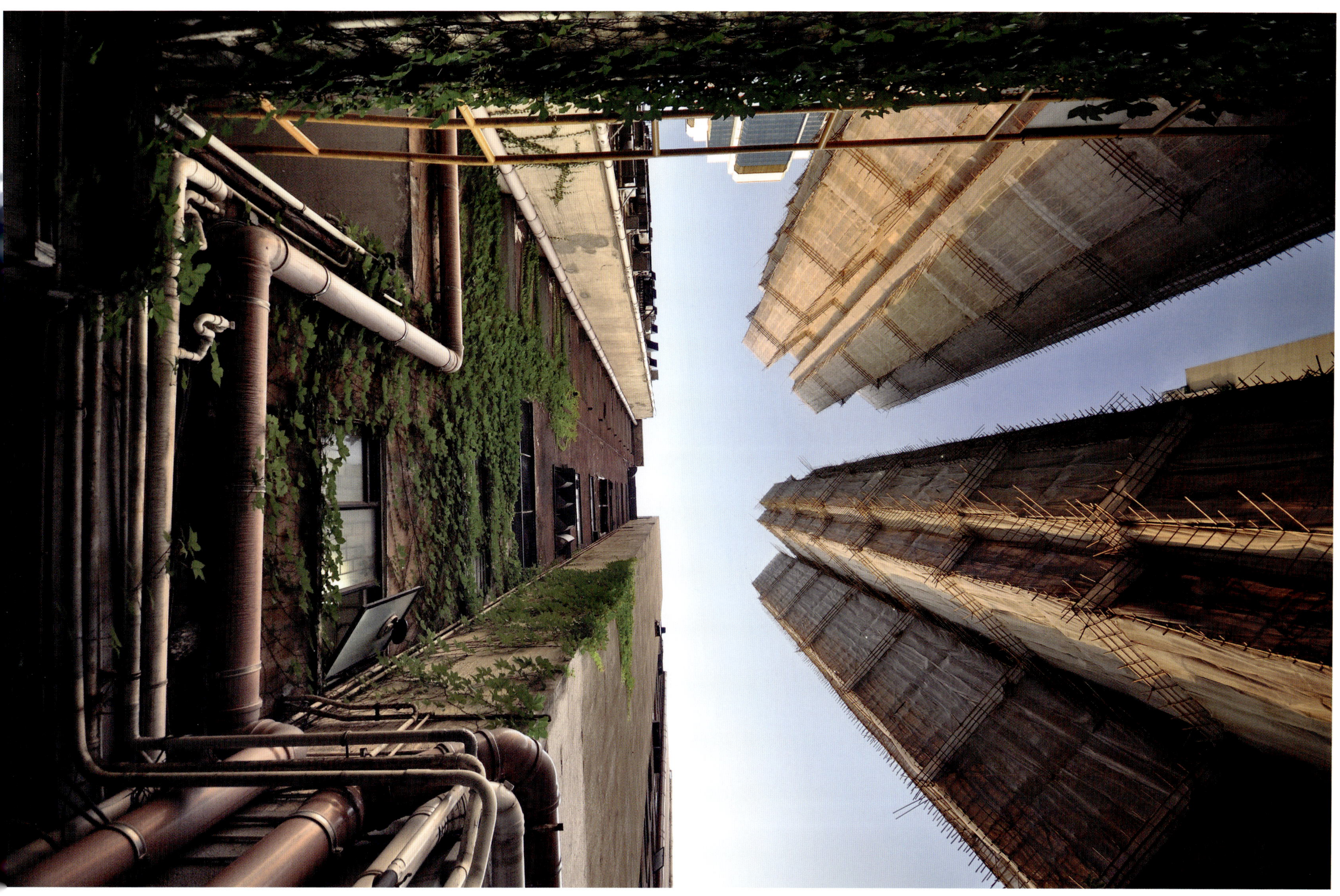

興建

Development

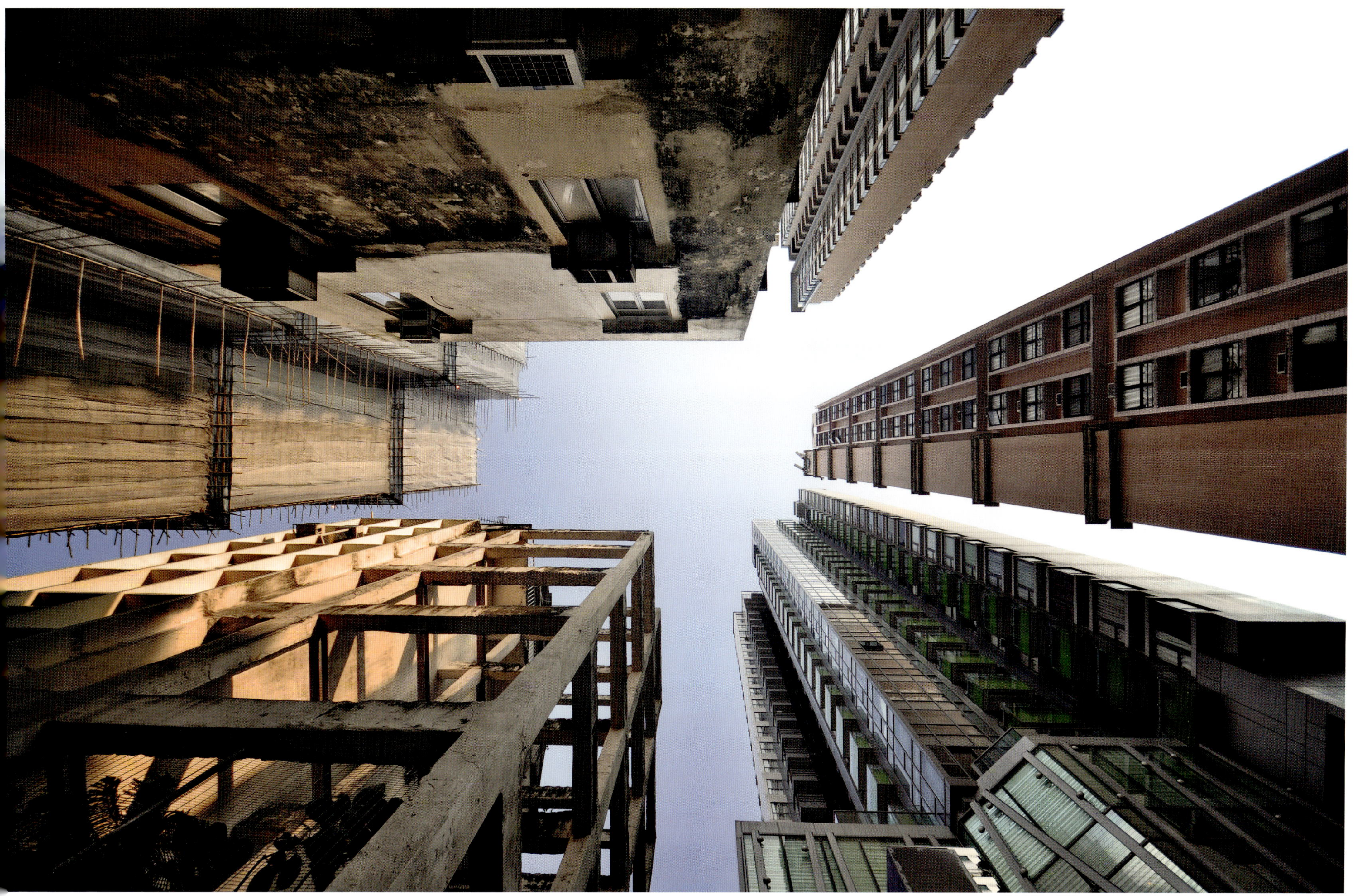

交織

Interwoven

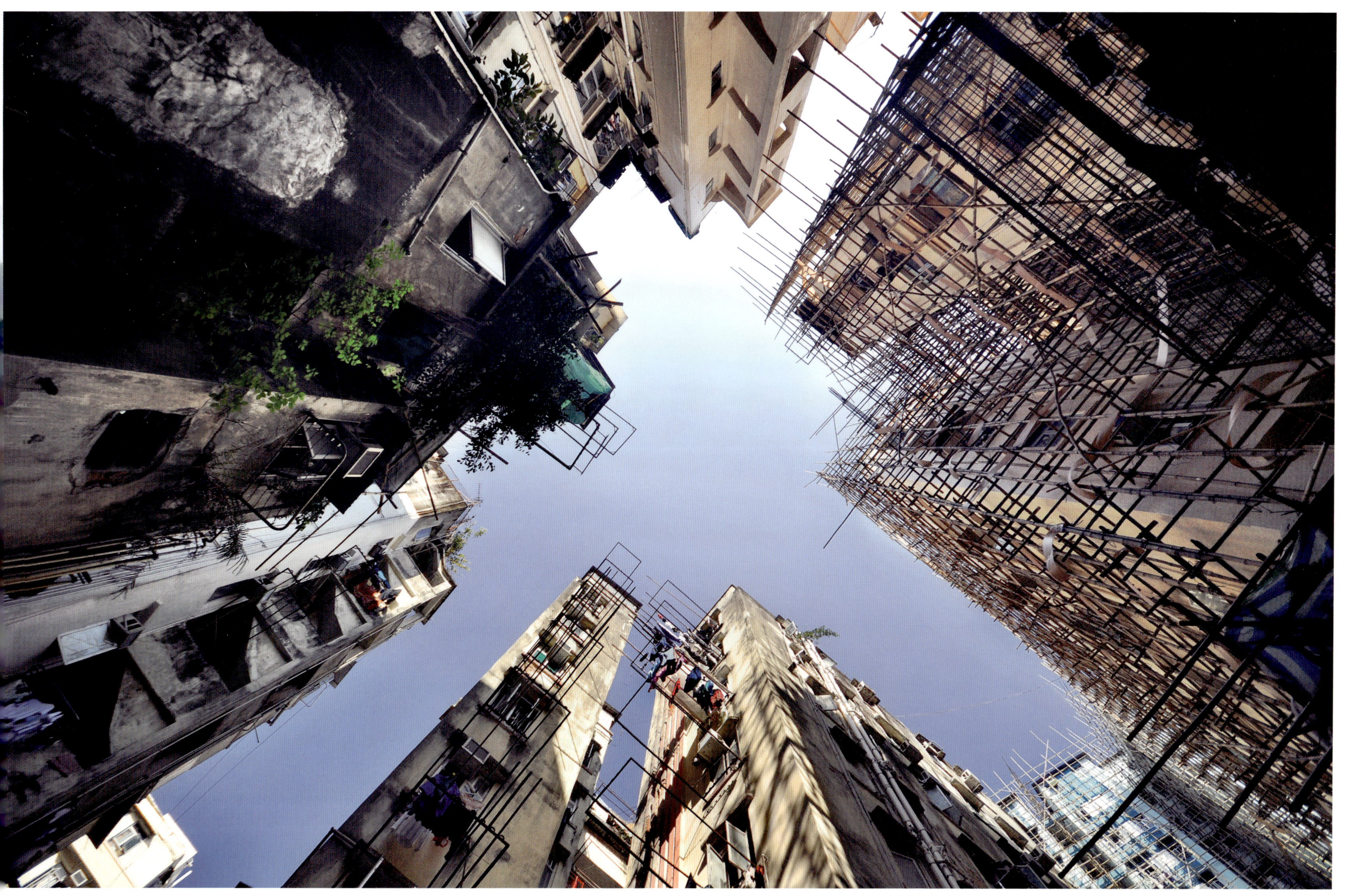

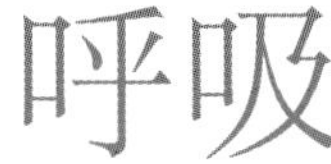

呼吸

Breath

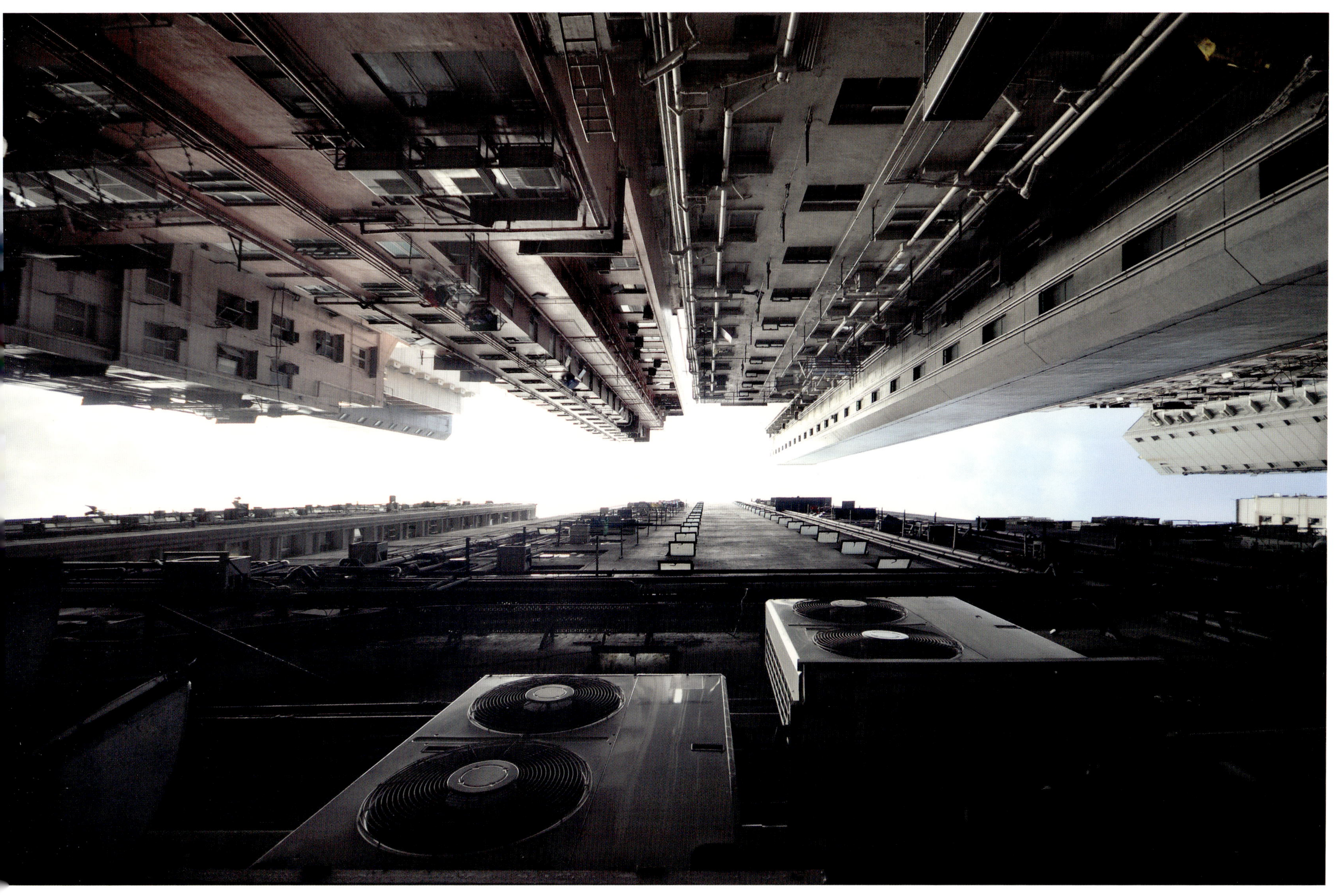

出路

Way Out

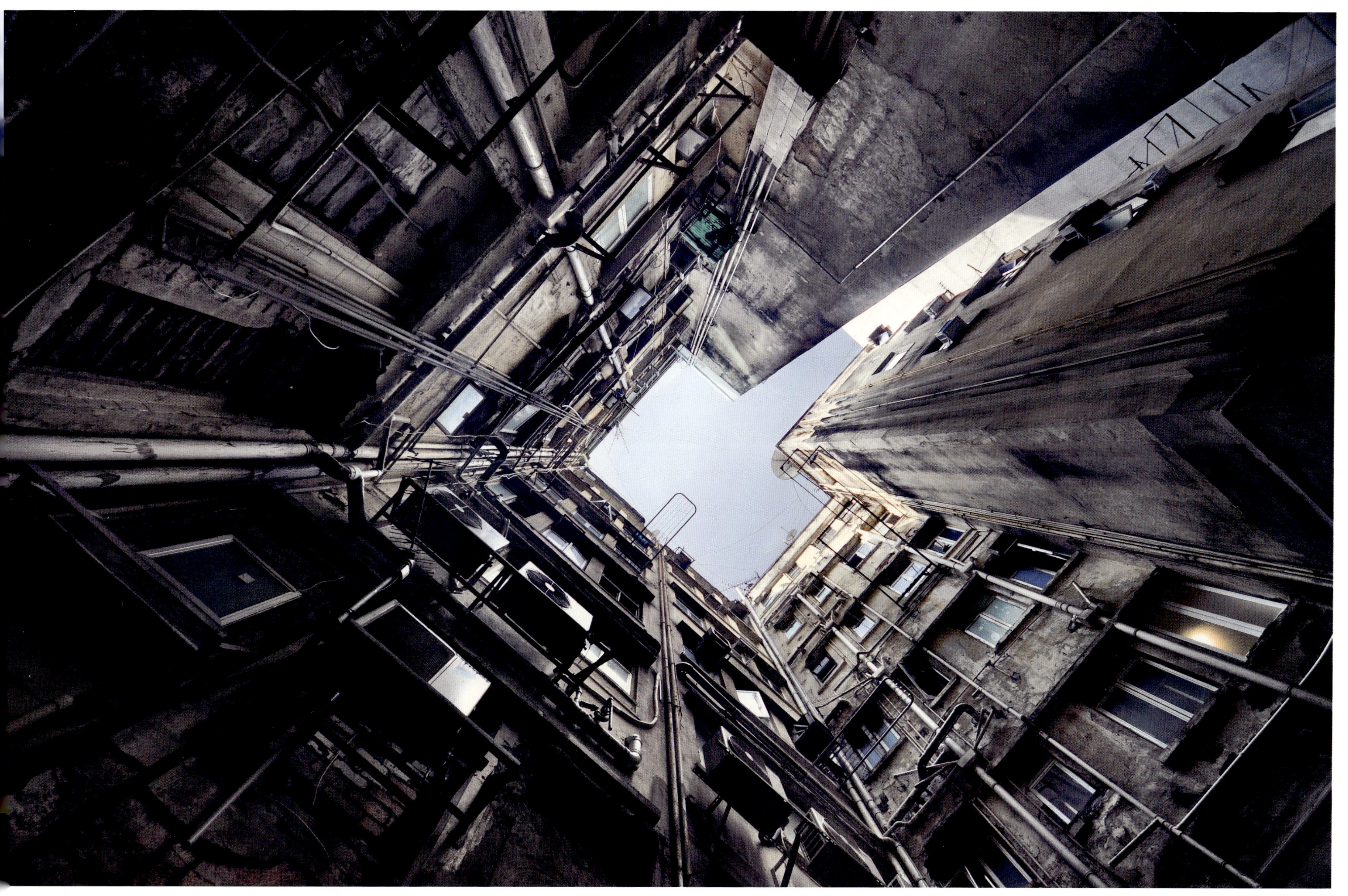

墜落

Fall

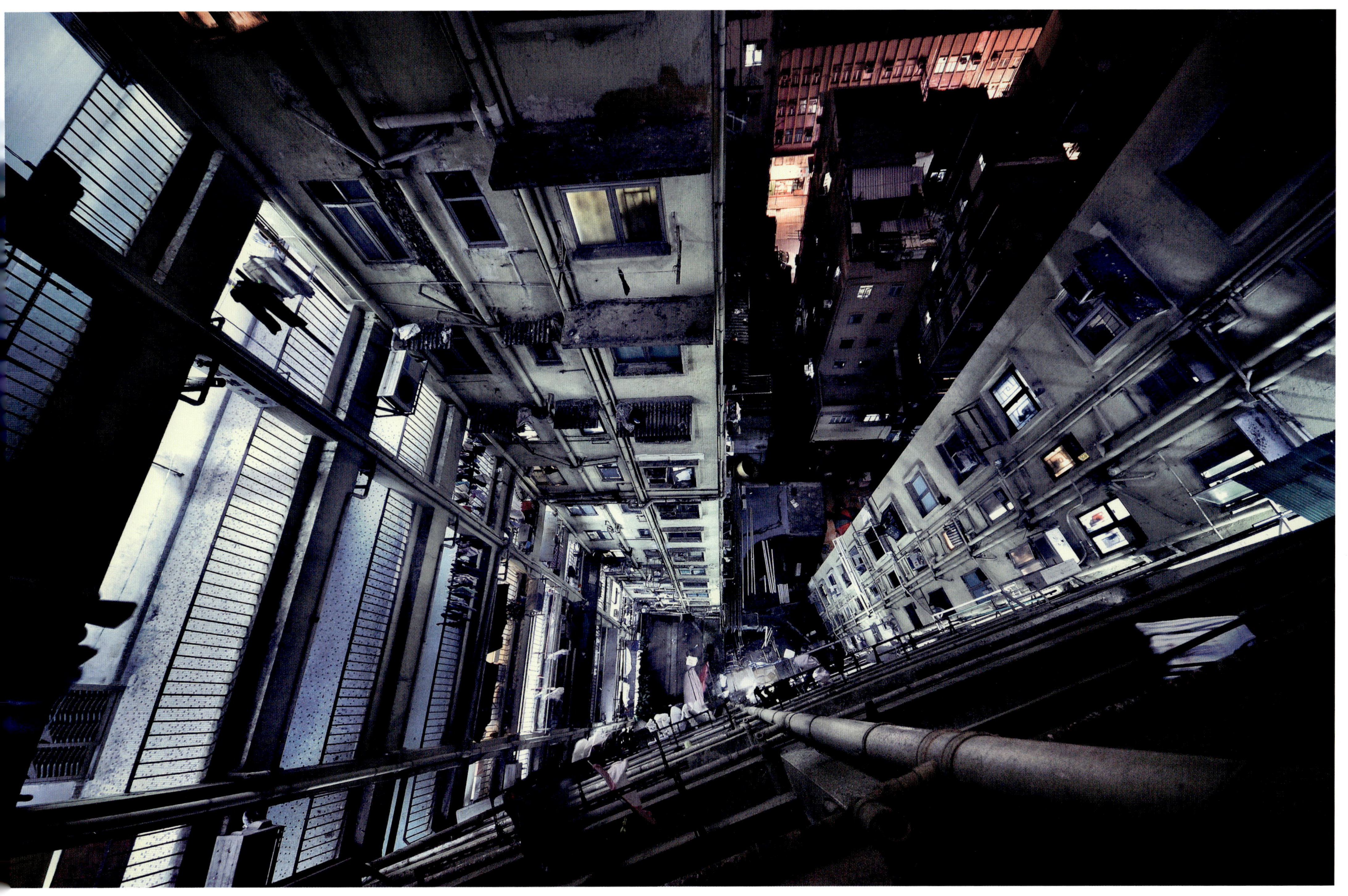

紛紜雜沓

Clutter

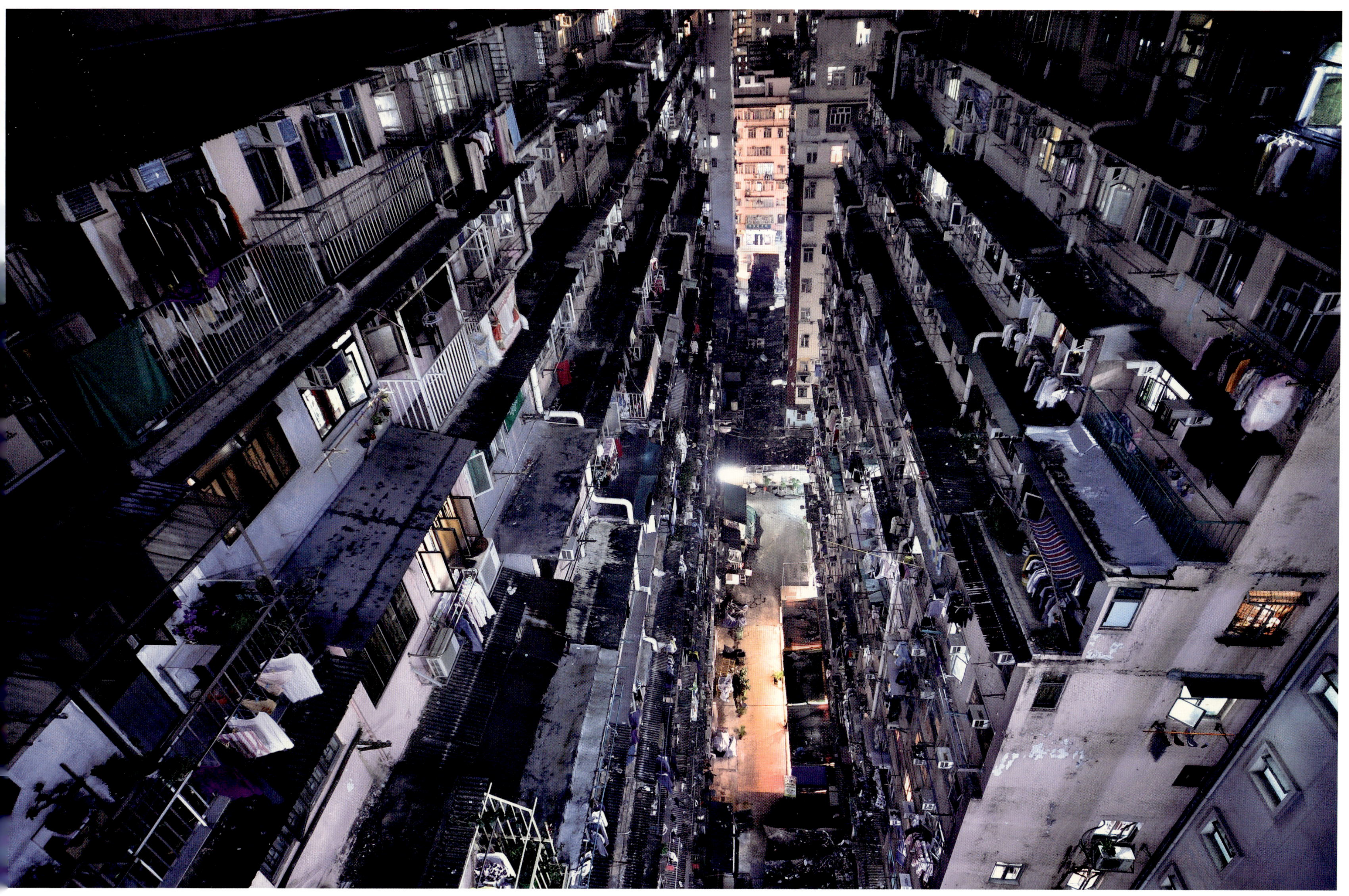

井然有序

Regularity

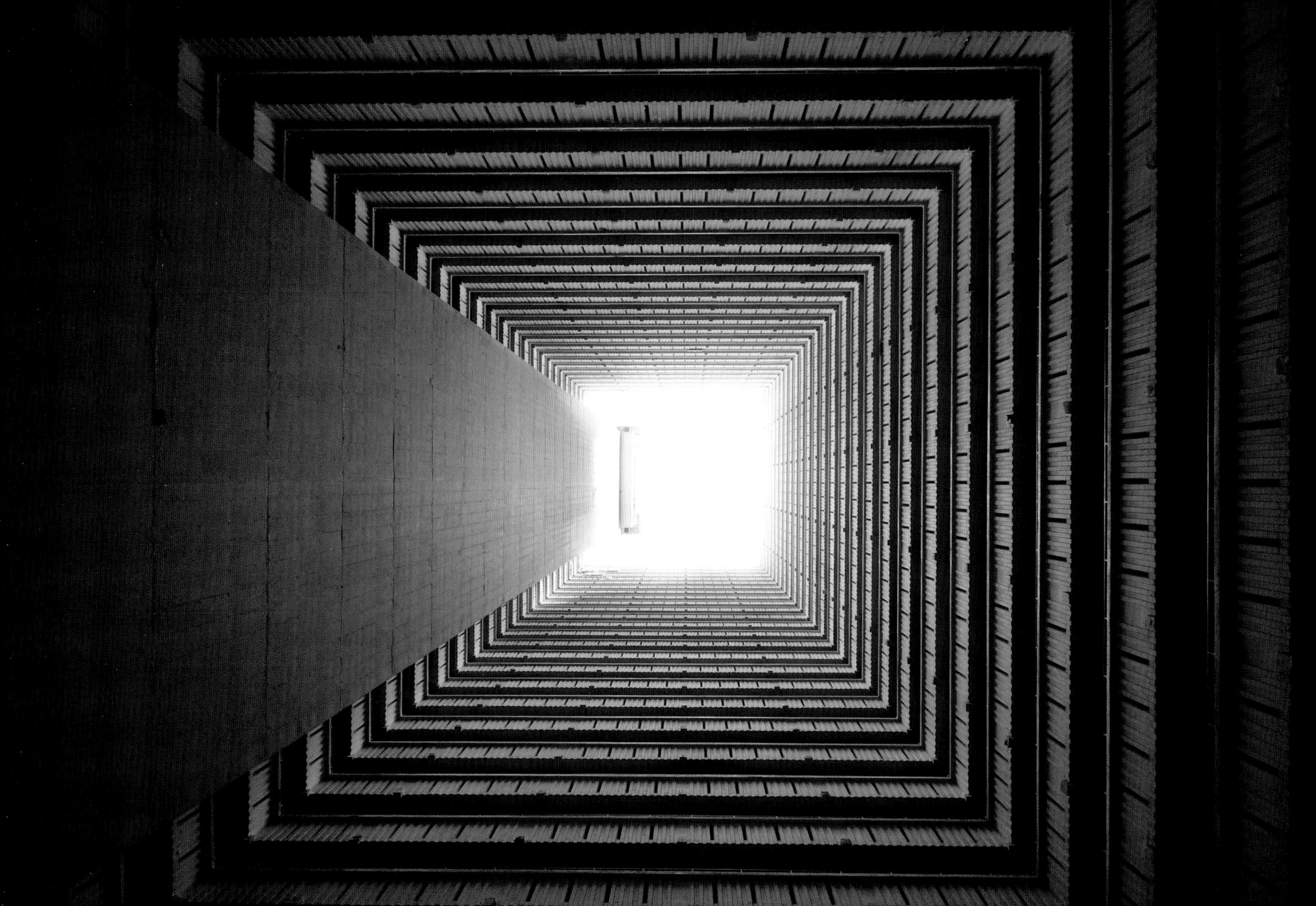

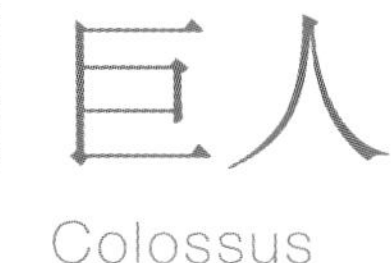

巨人

Colossus

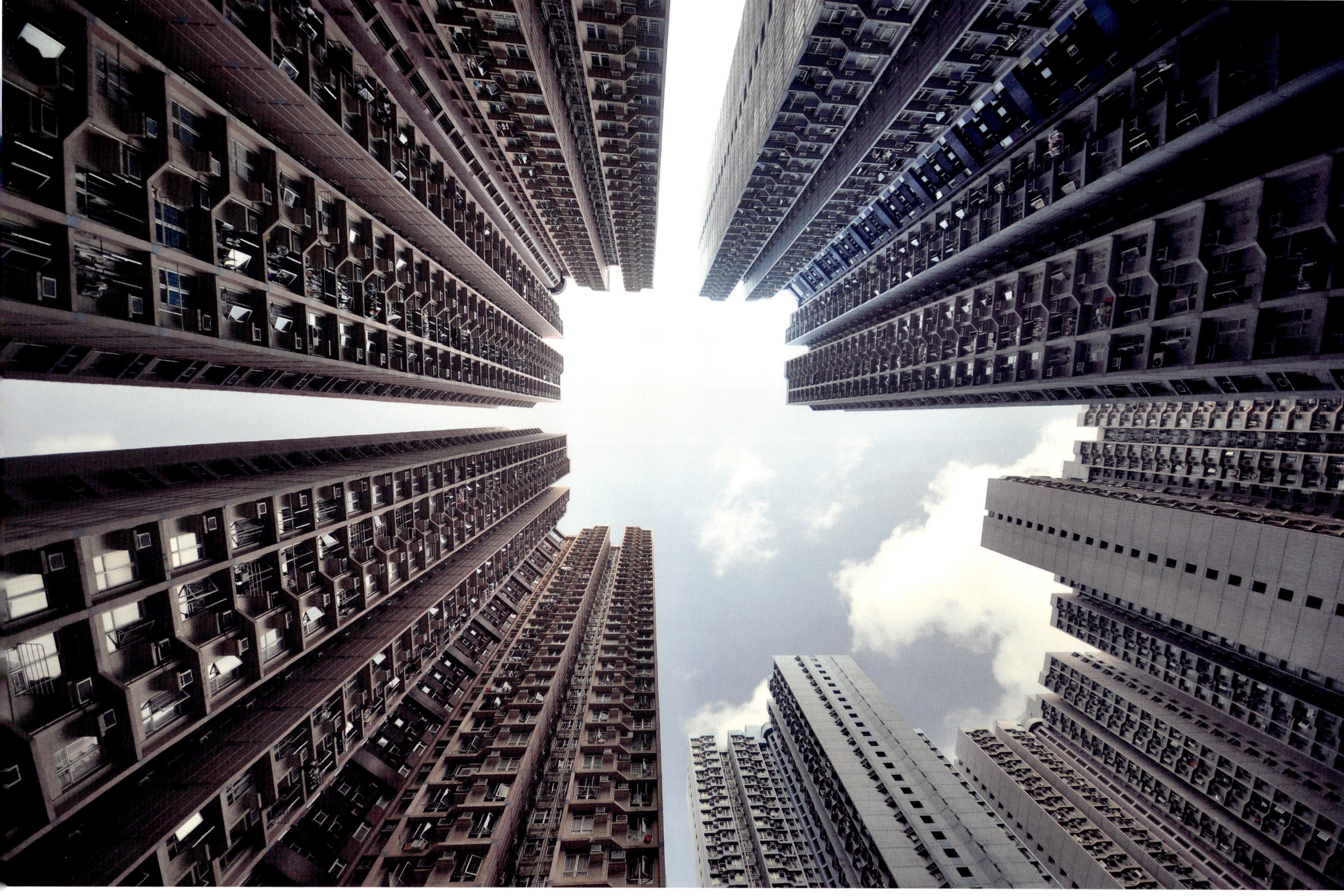

天梯

Skyward

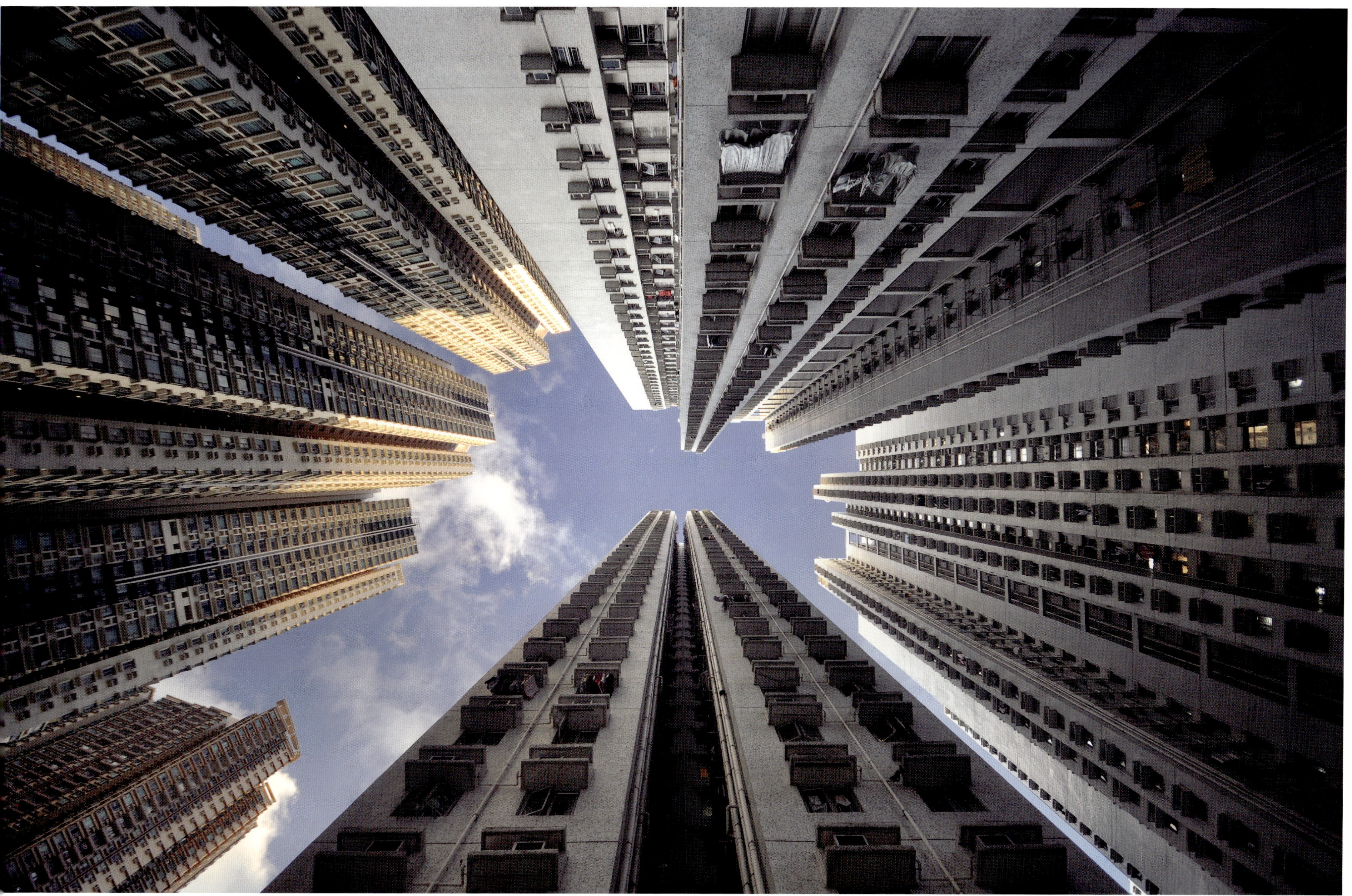

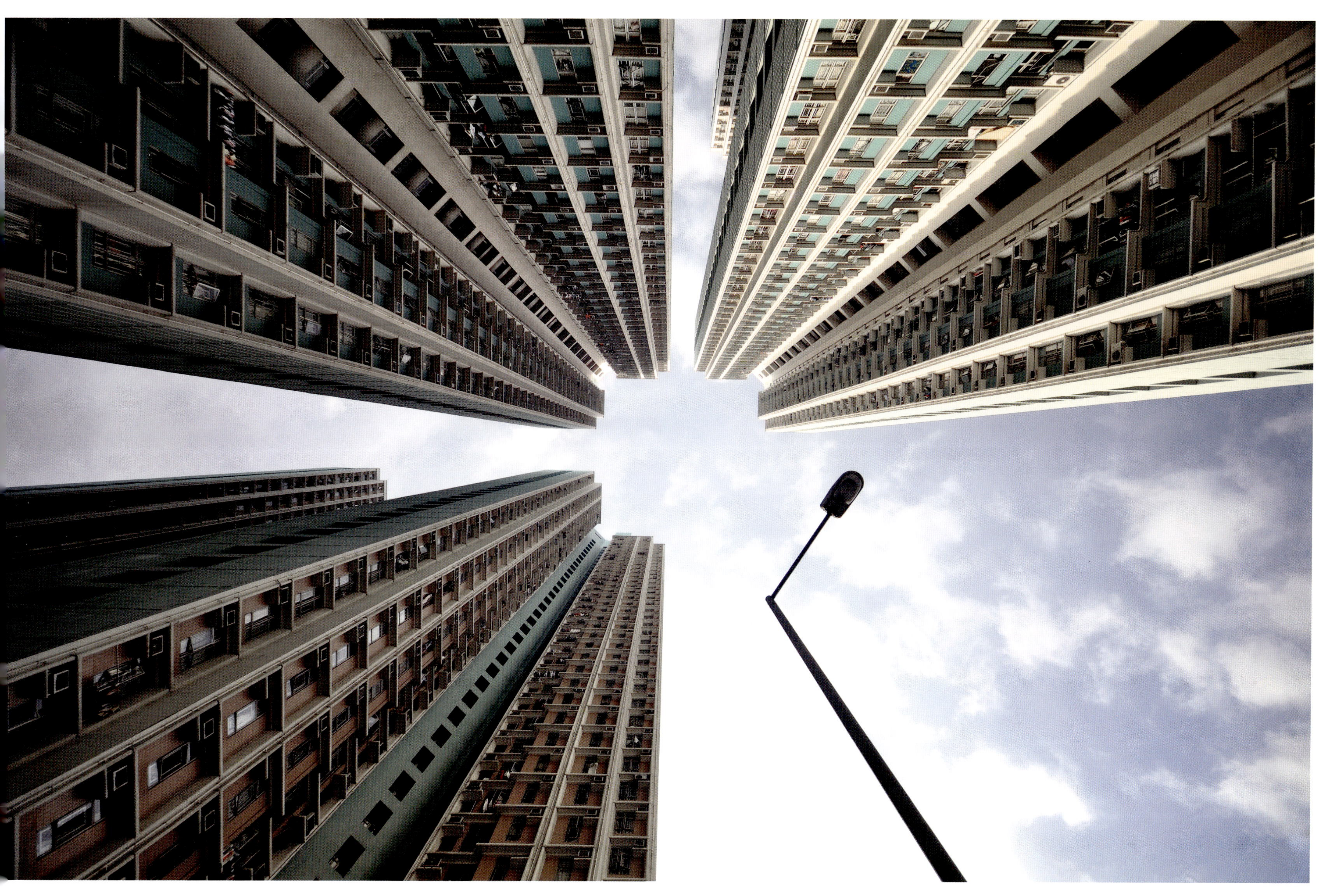

迴響

Echoes

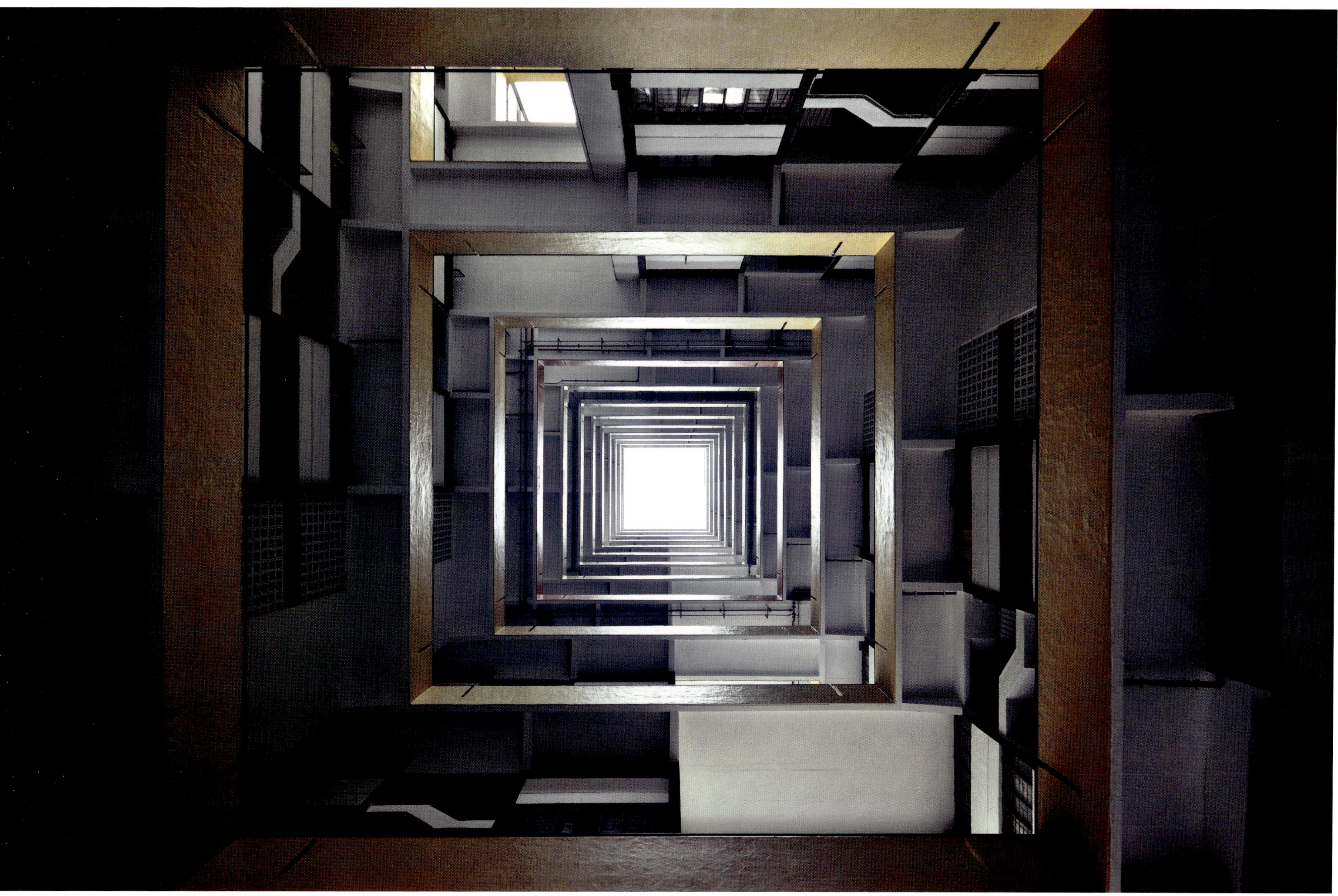

井

Well

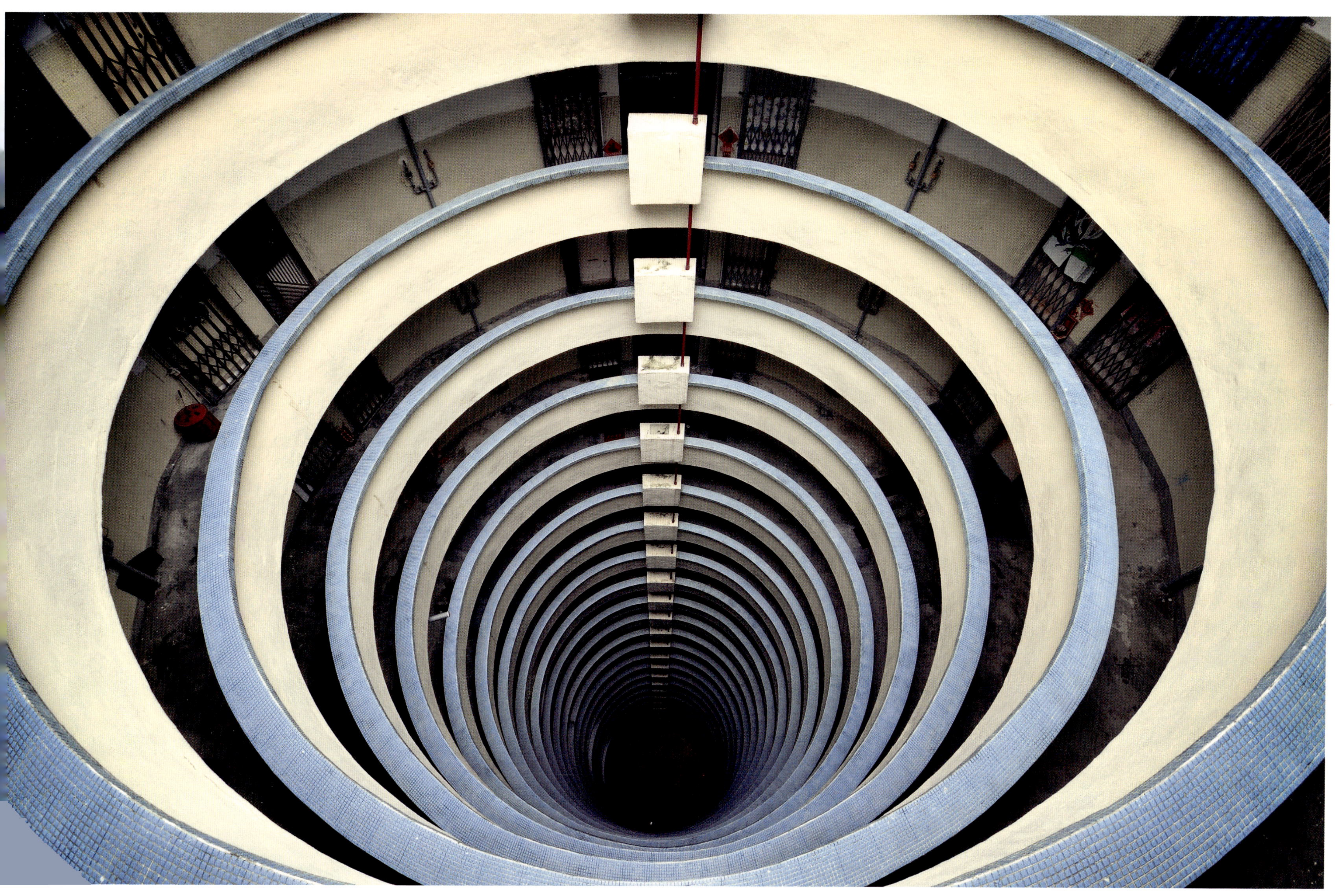

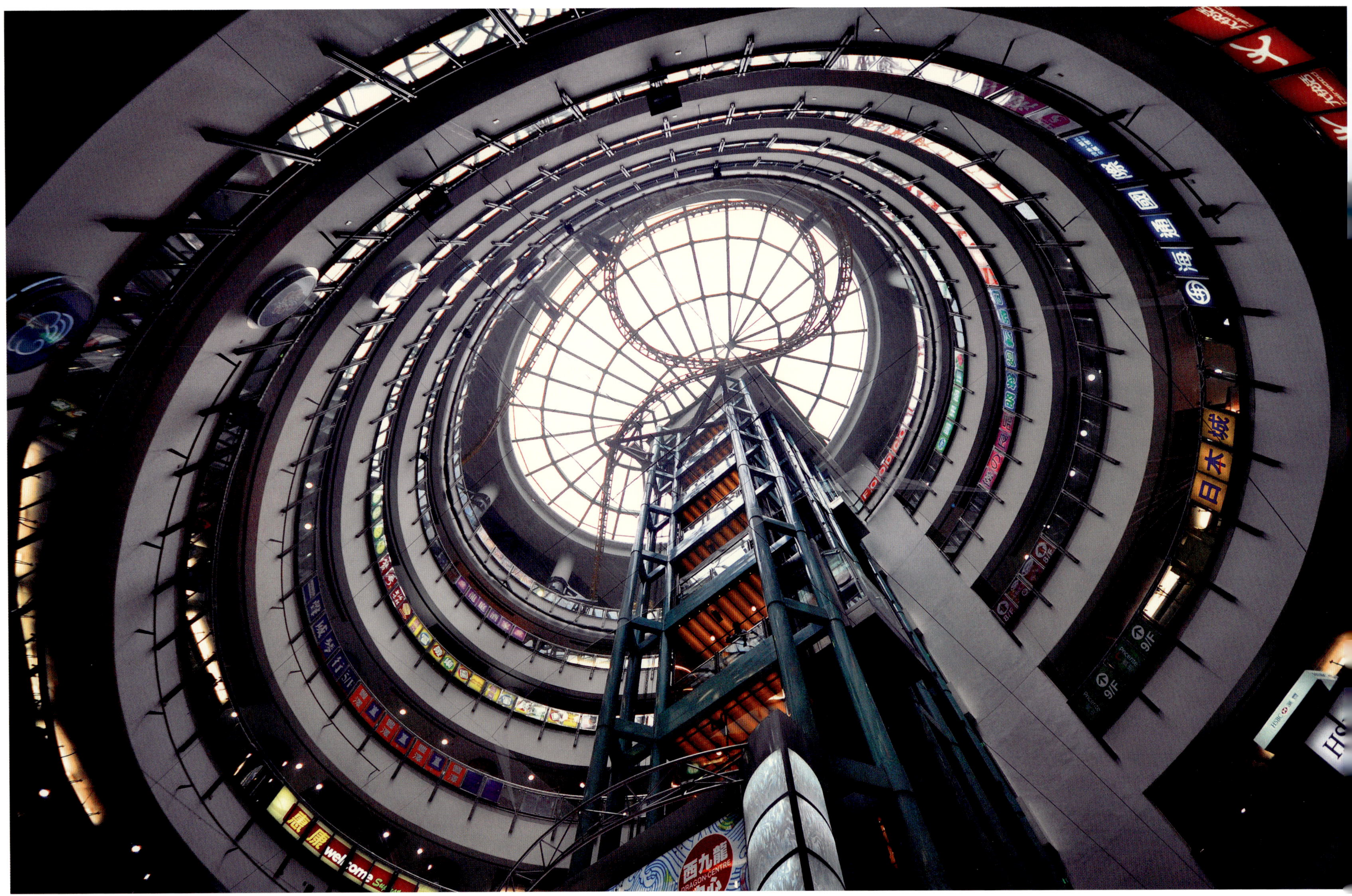
日本城
西九龍
DRAGON·CENTRE

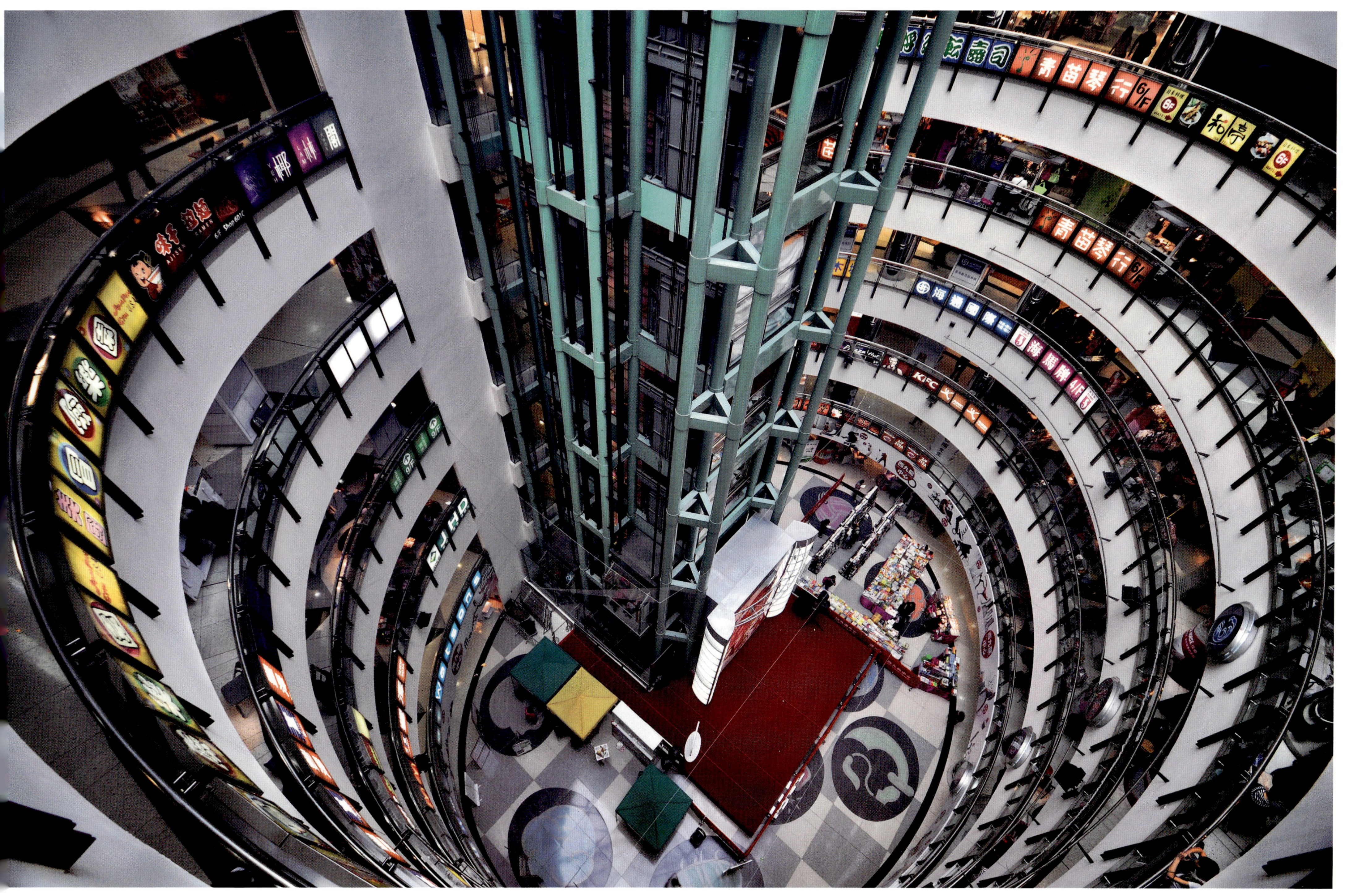

壽司
青苗琴行 6/F
6F
和亭
6F
青苗琴行 6/F
海馬牌 4/F
KFC

交易
Exchange

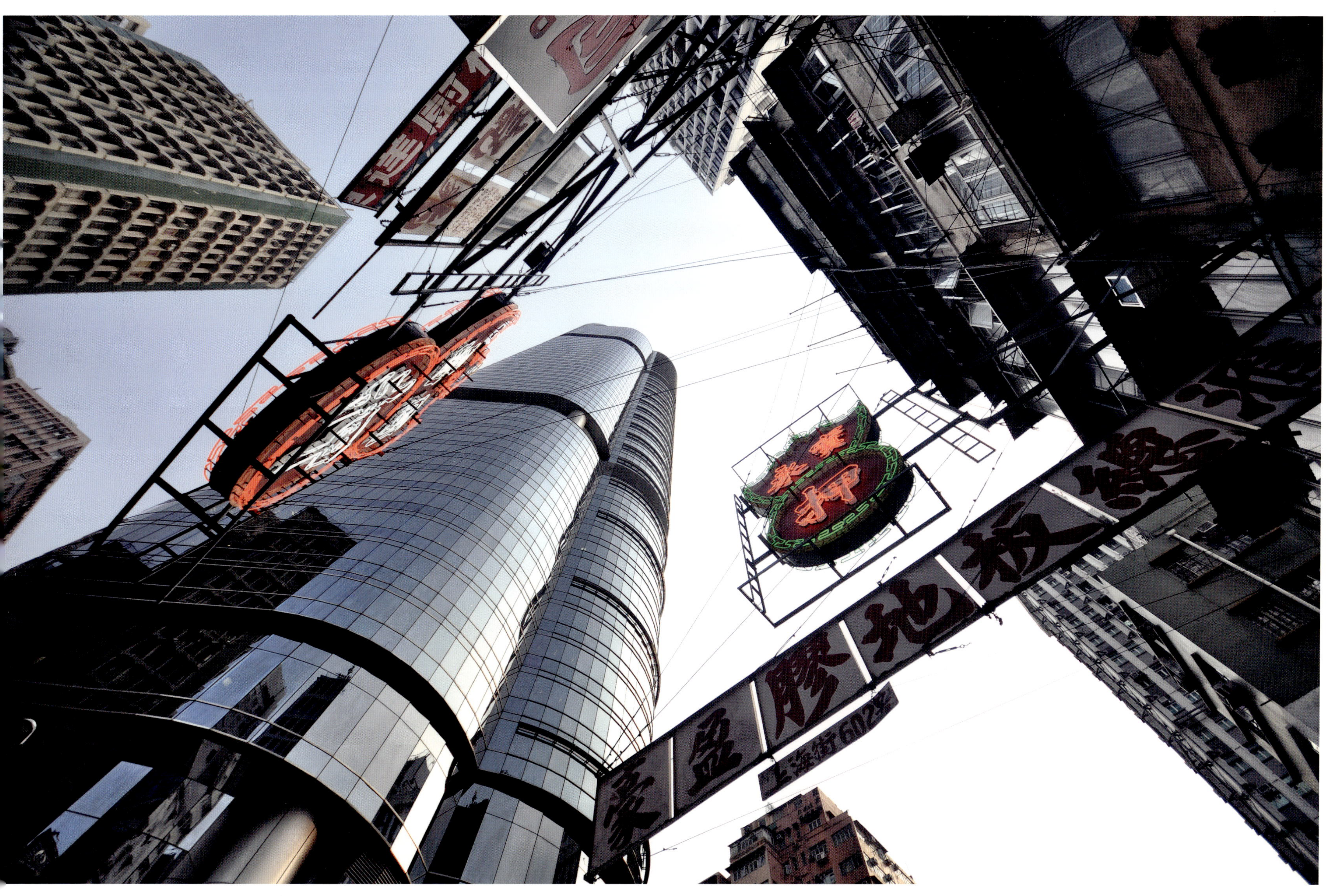

豪盈膠地板
上海街602號
押

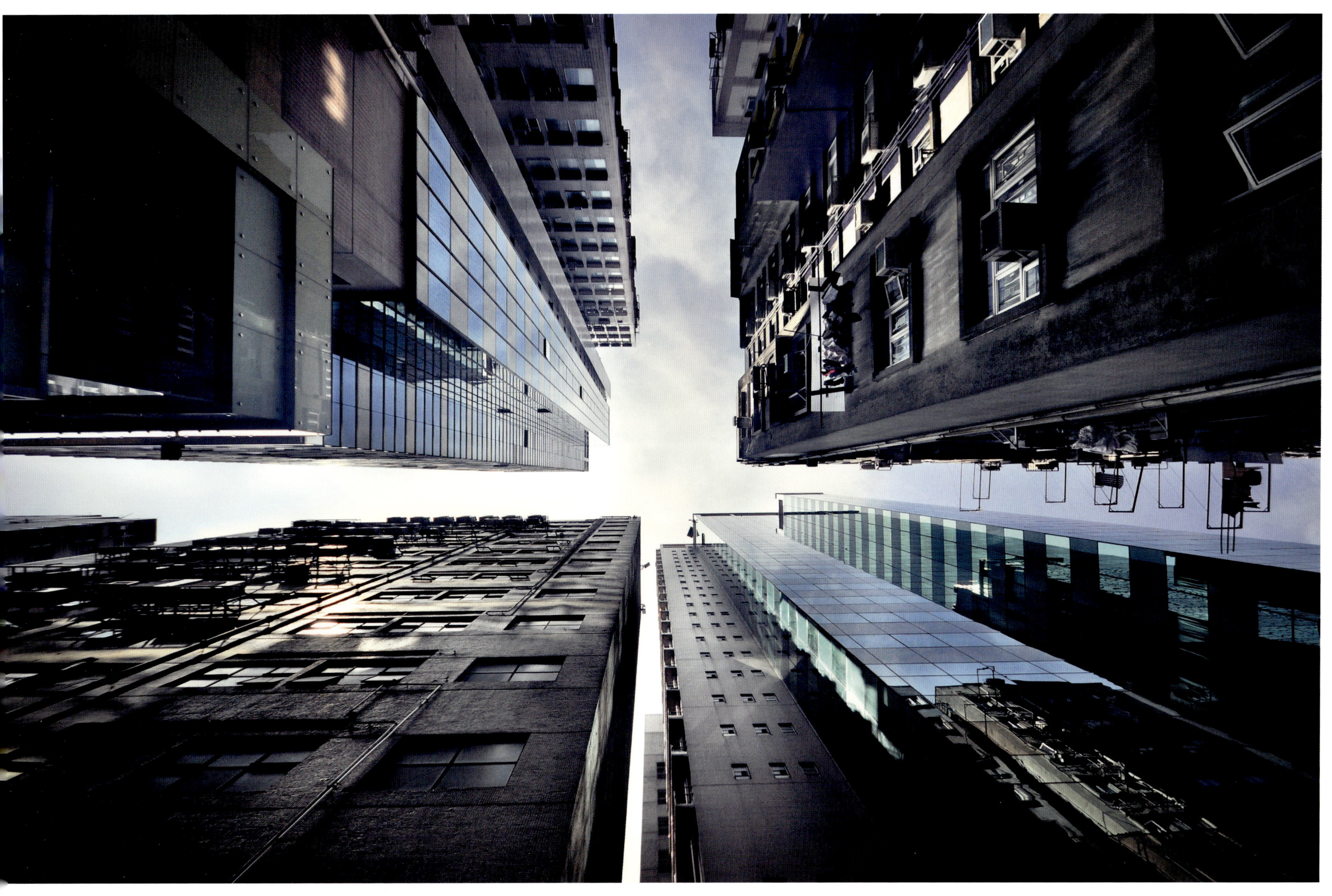

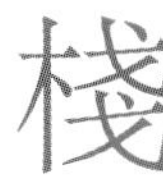

Inn

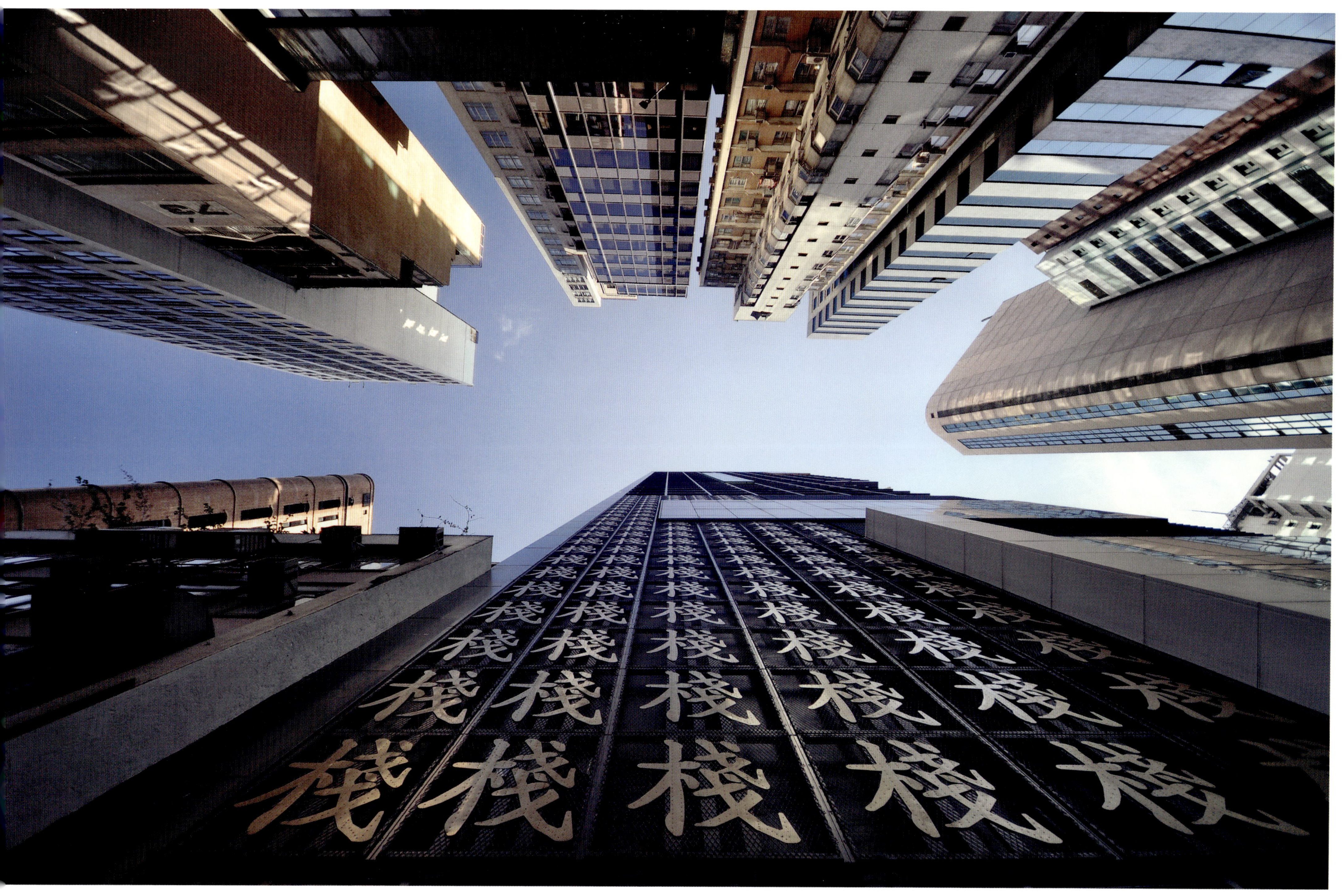
棧

天網

Net

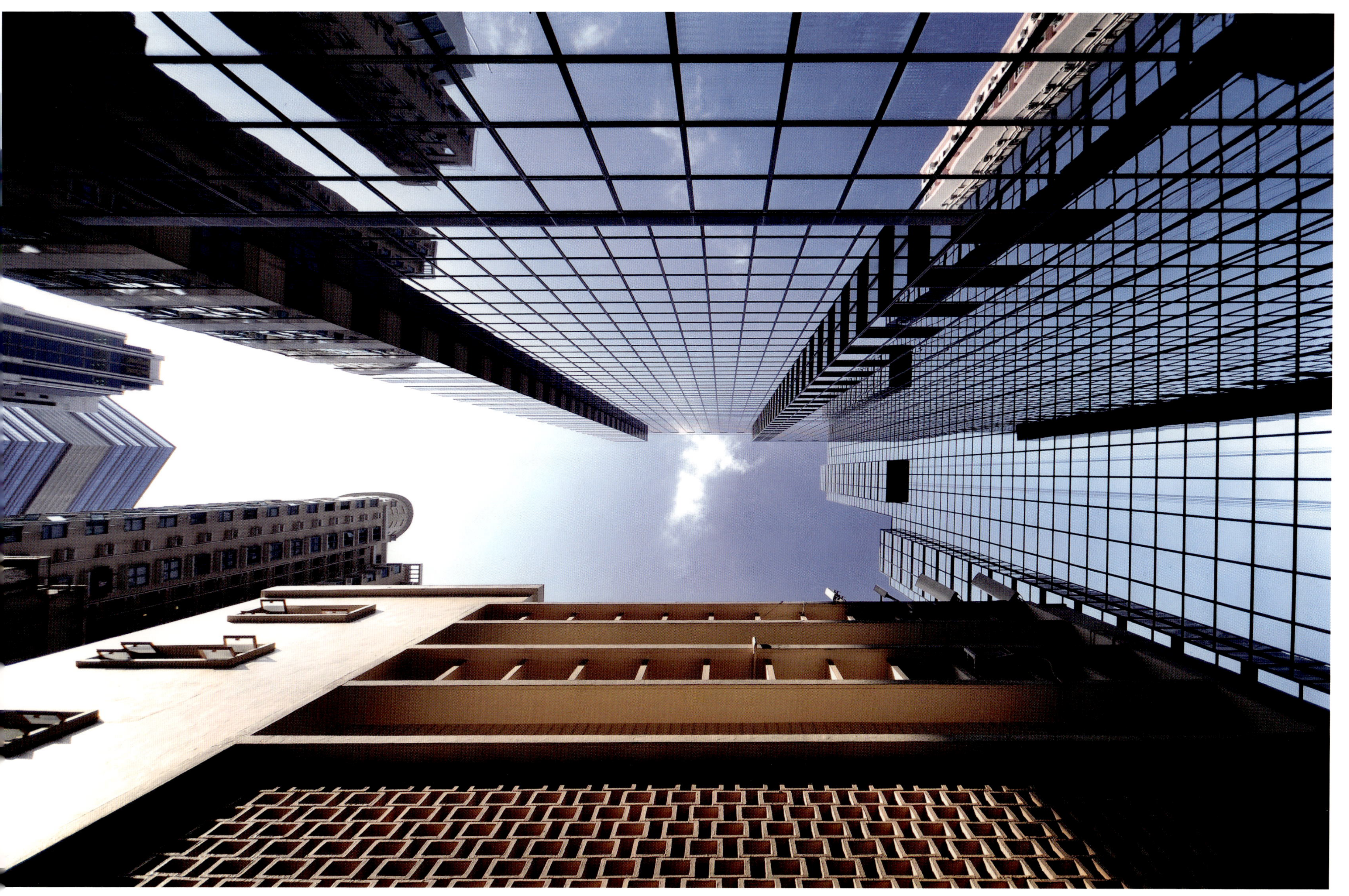

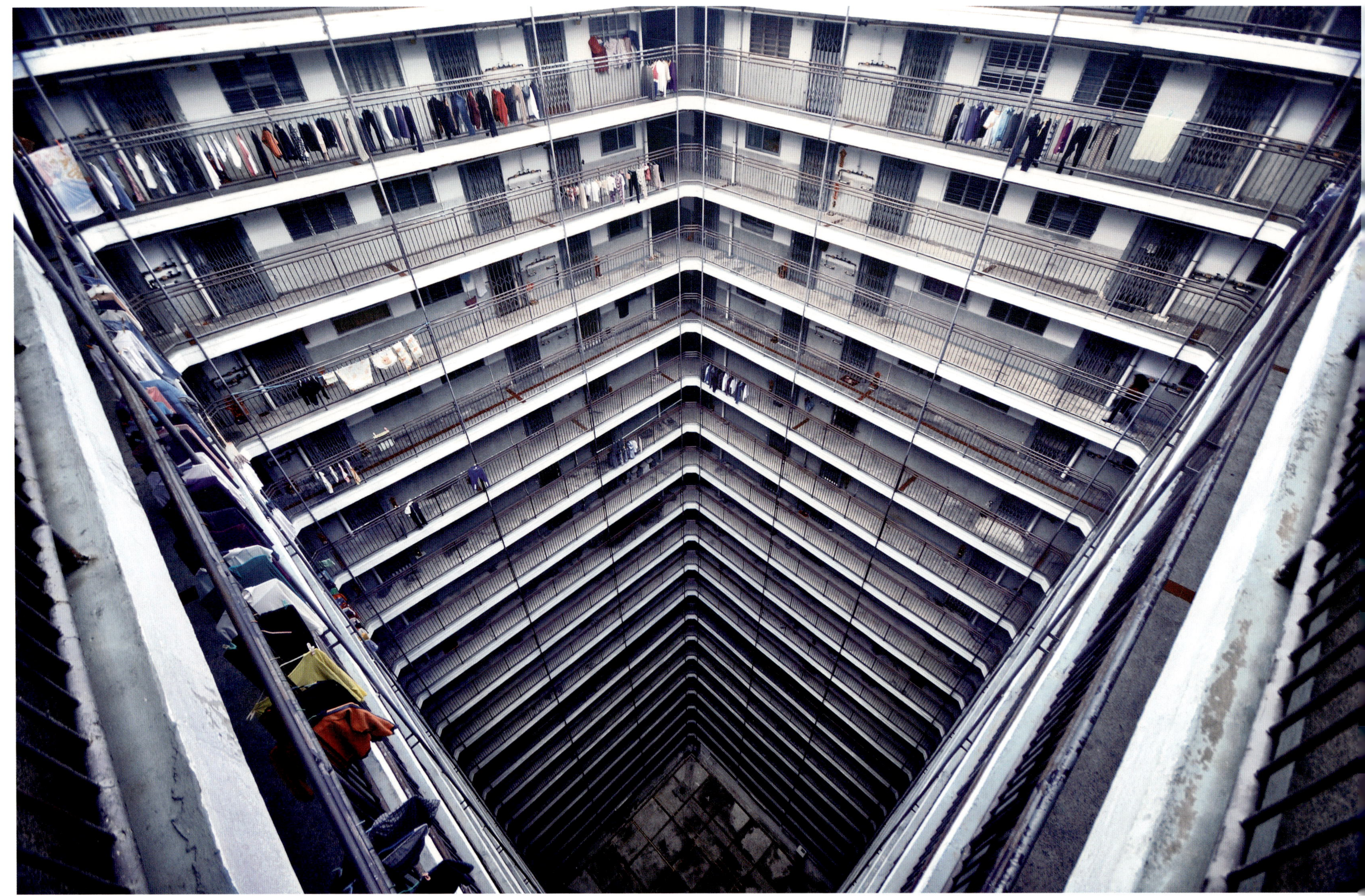

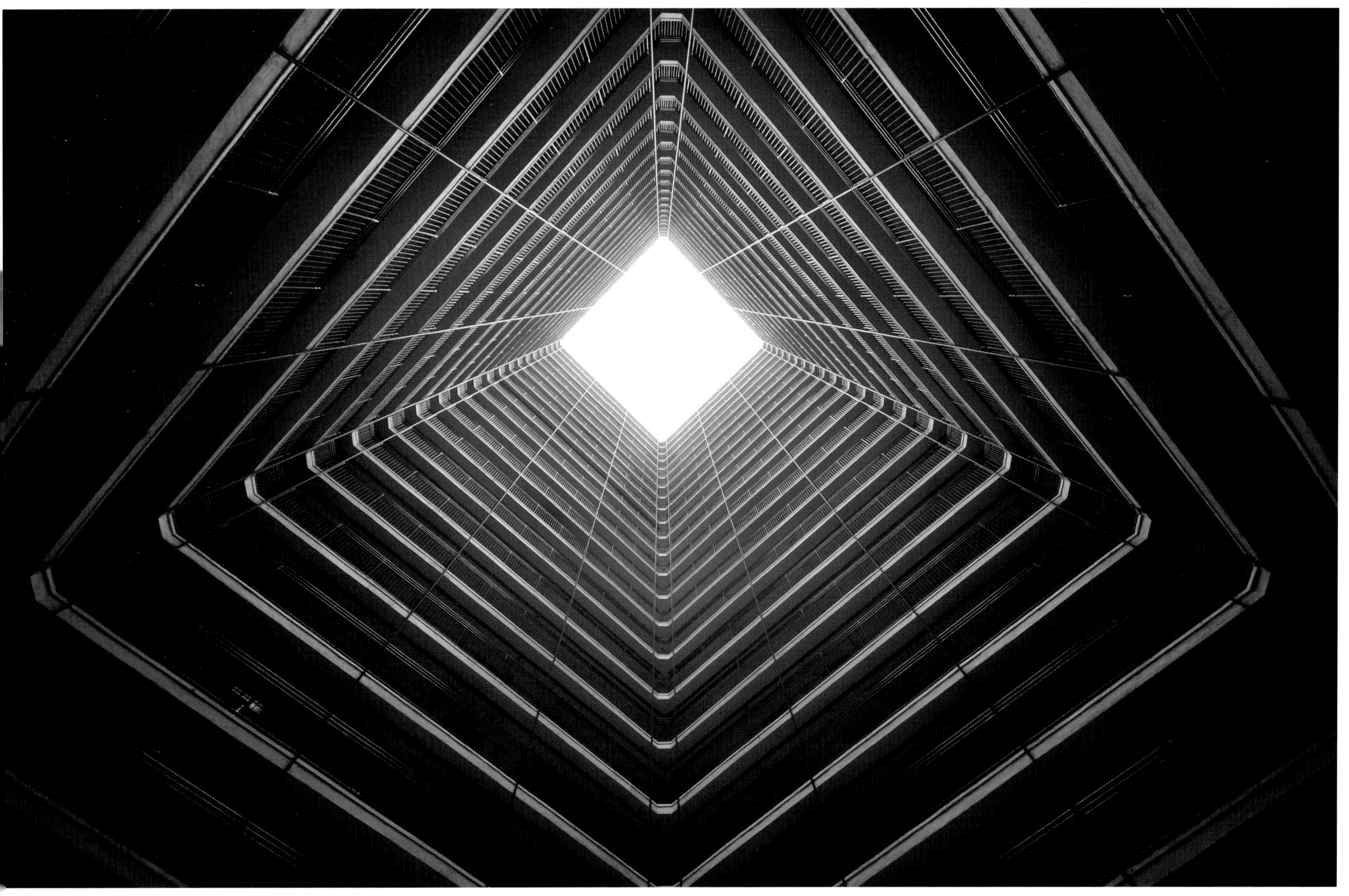

反射

Reflection

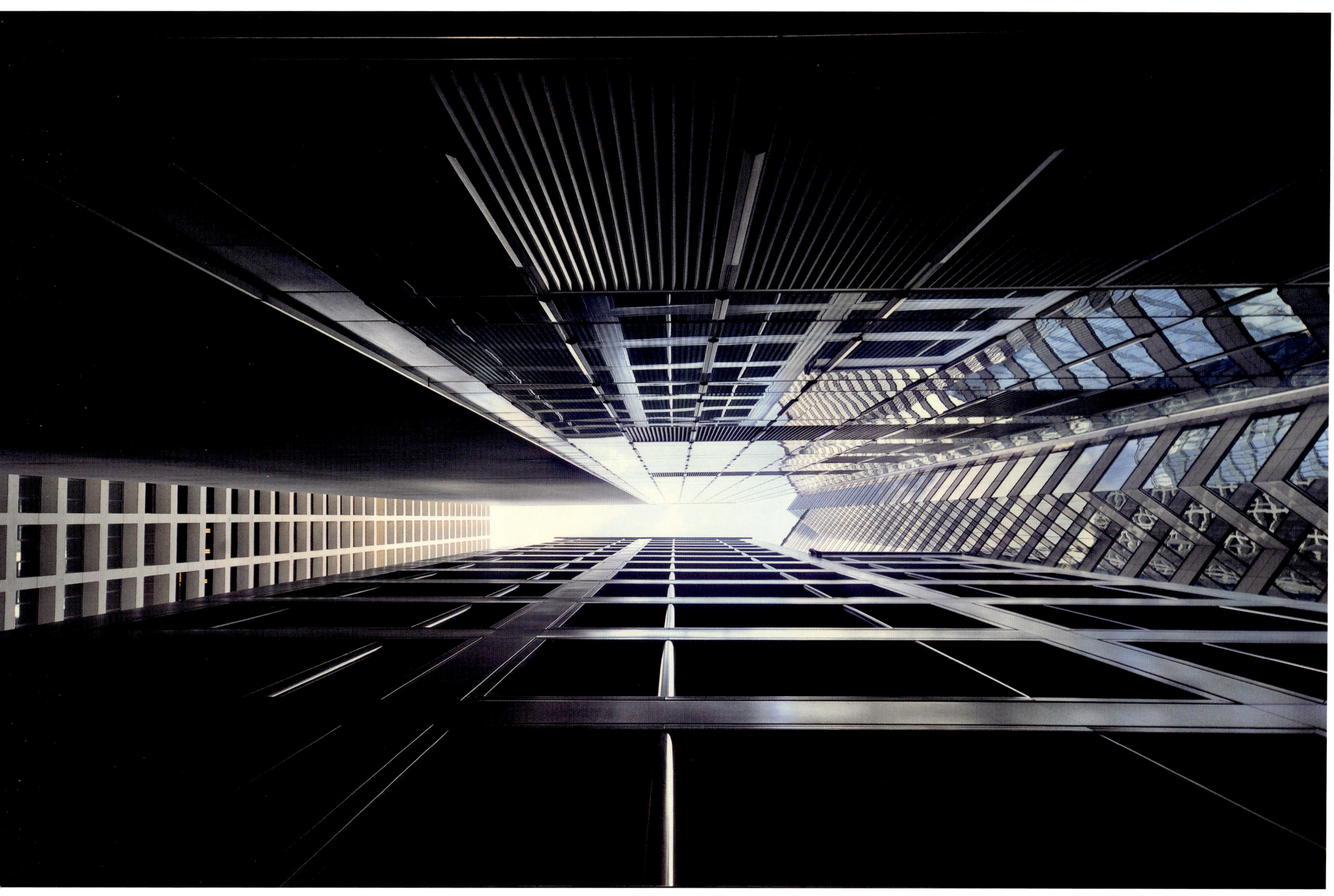

堅穩

Concrete

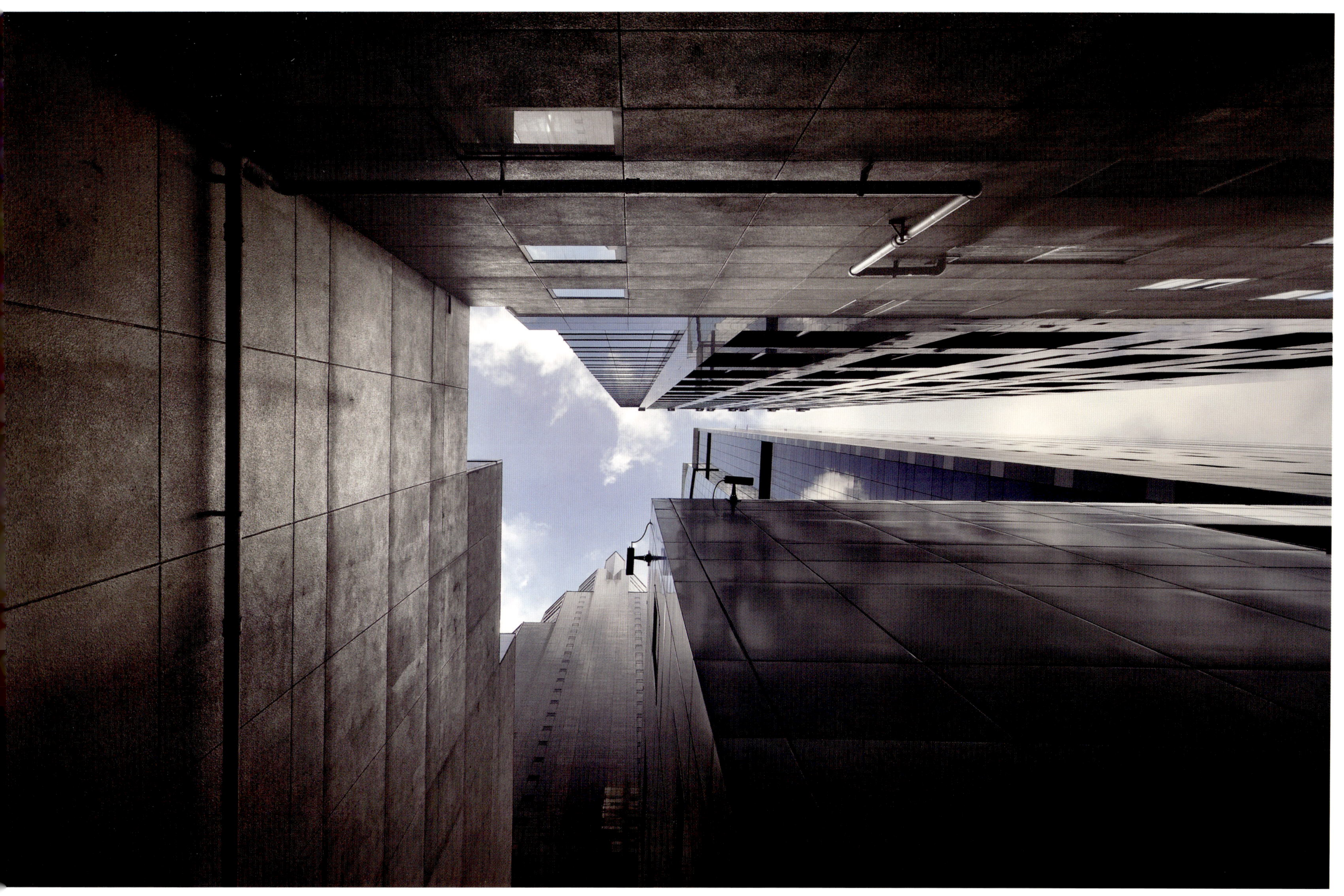

浮雲

Passing Clouds

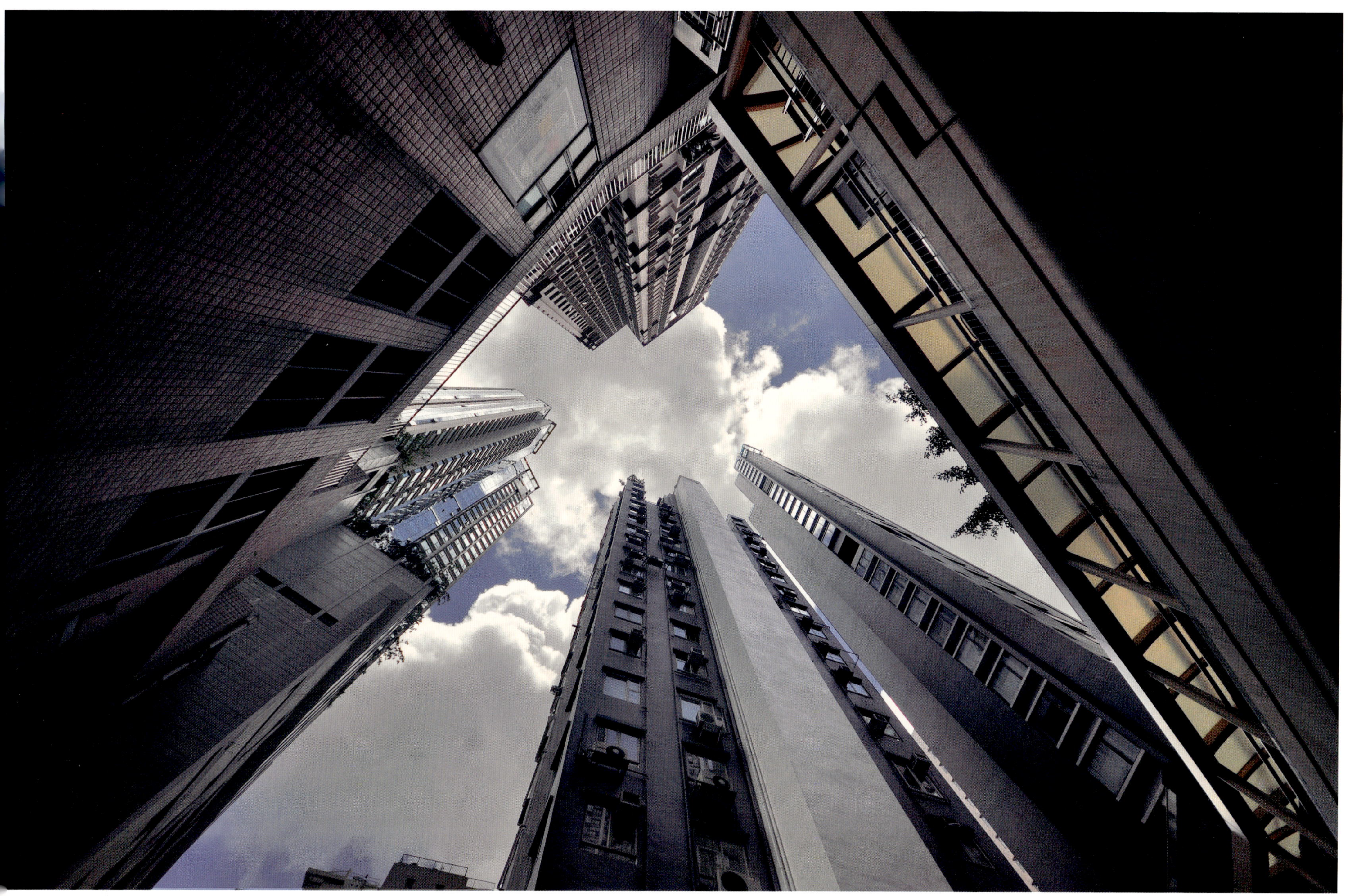

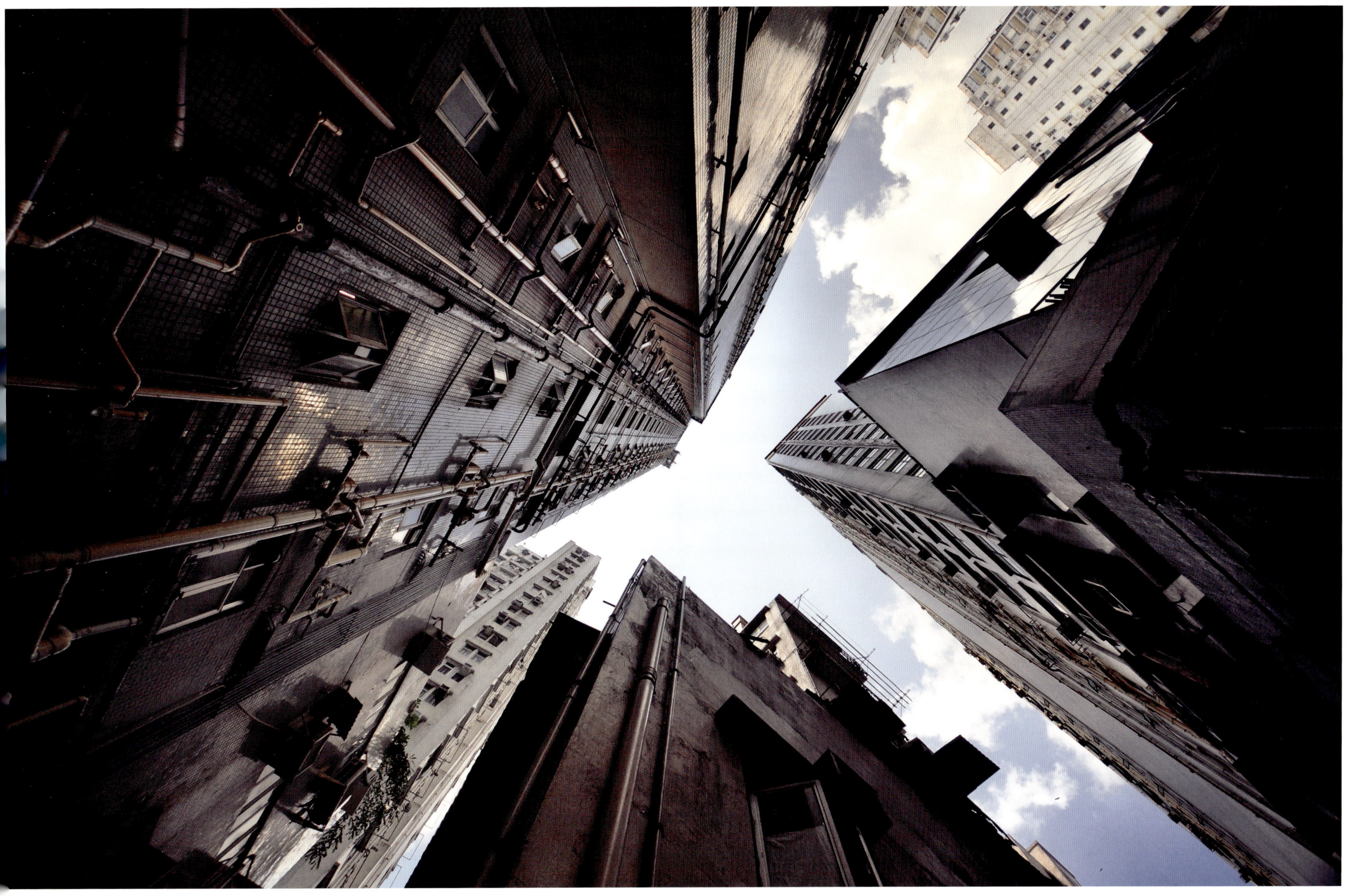

餘暉

Dim

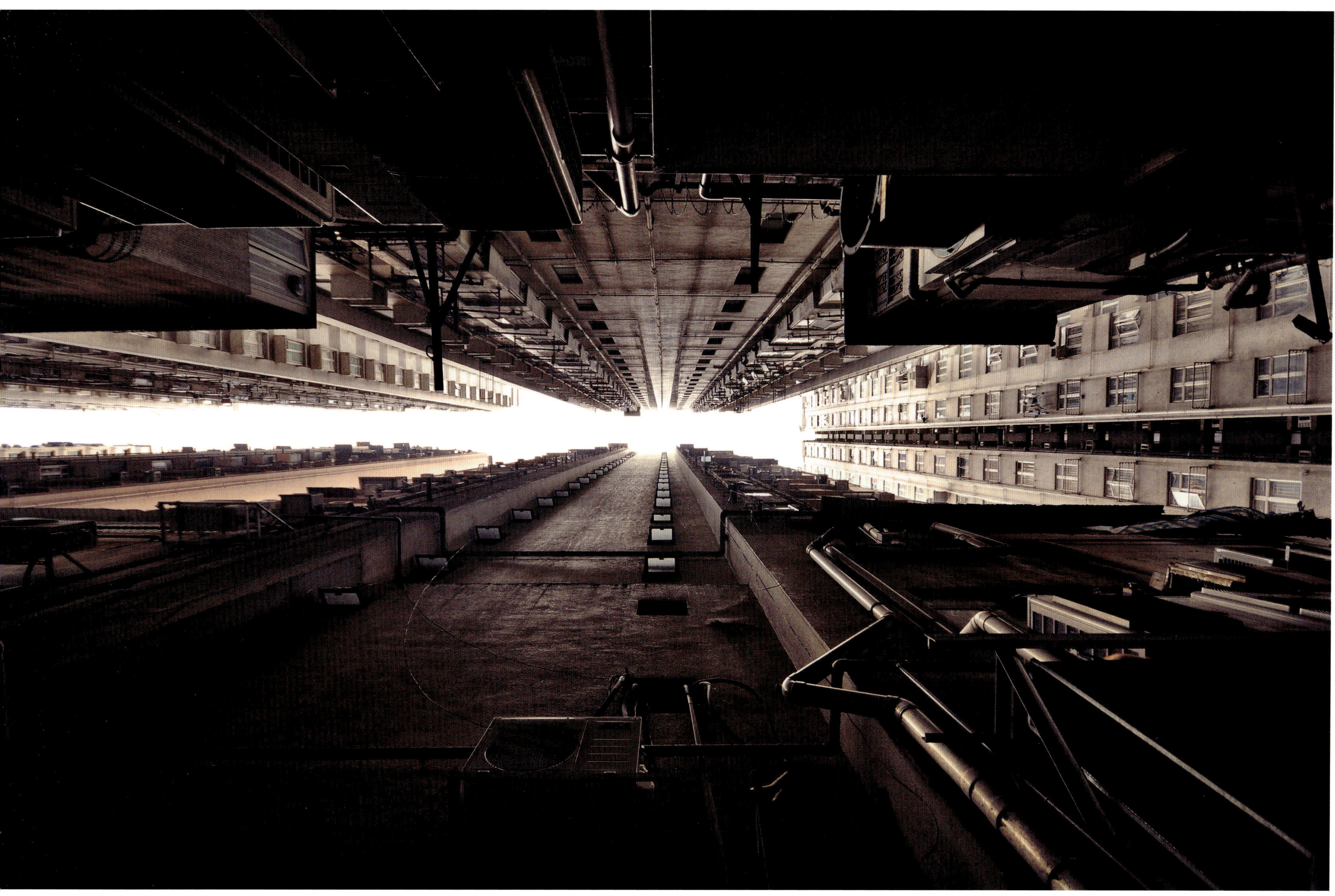

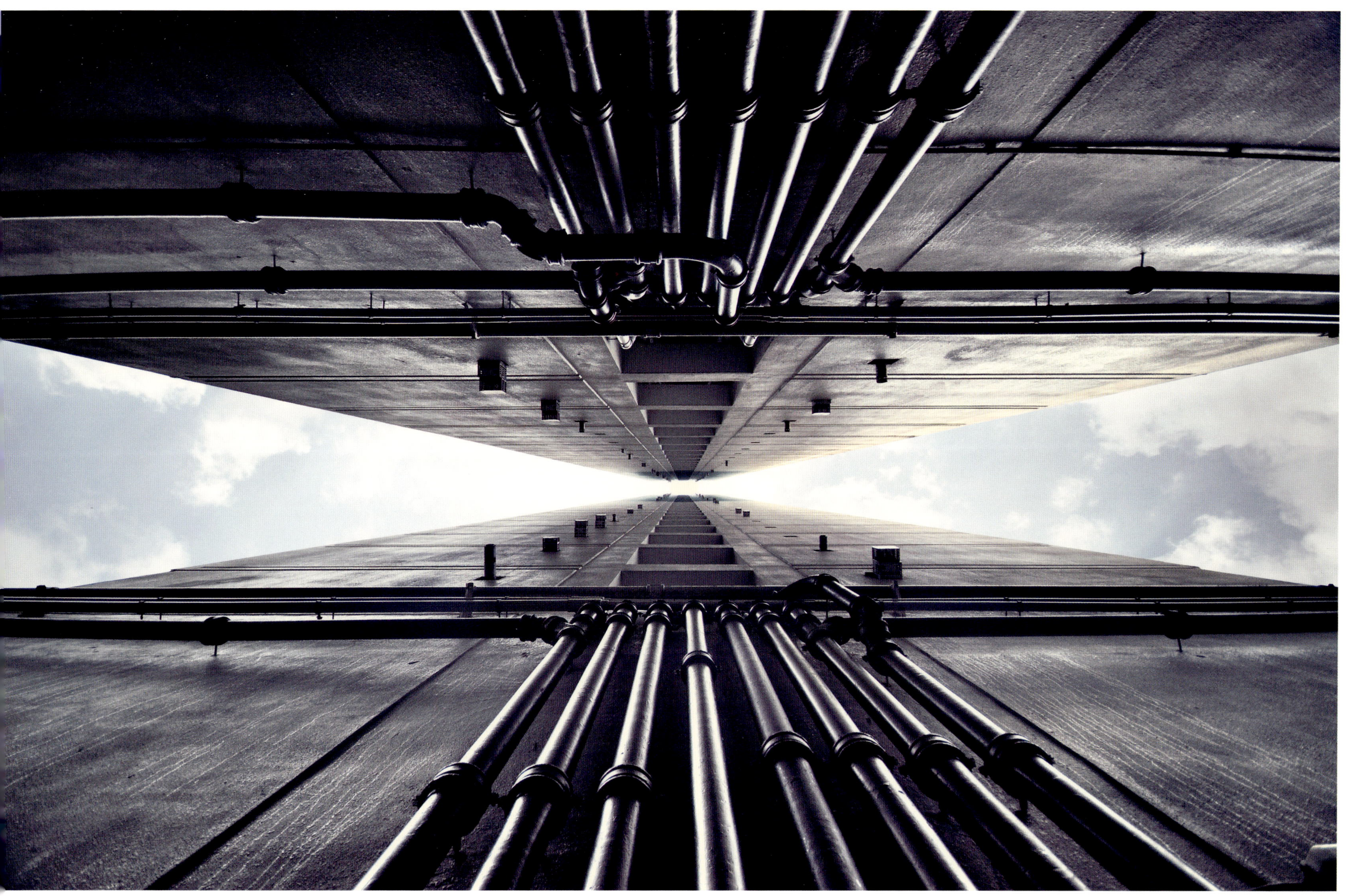

集合
Gathering

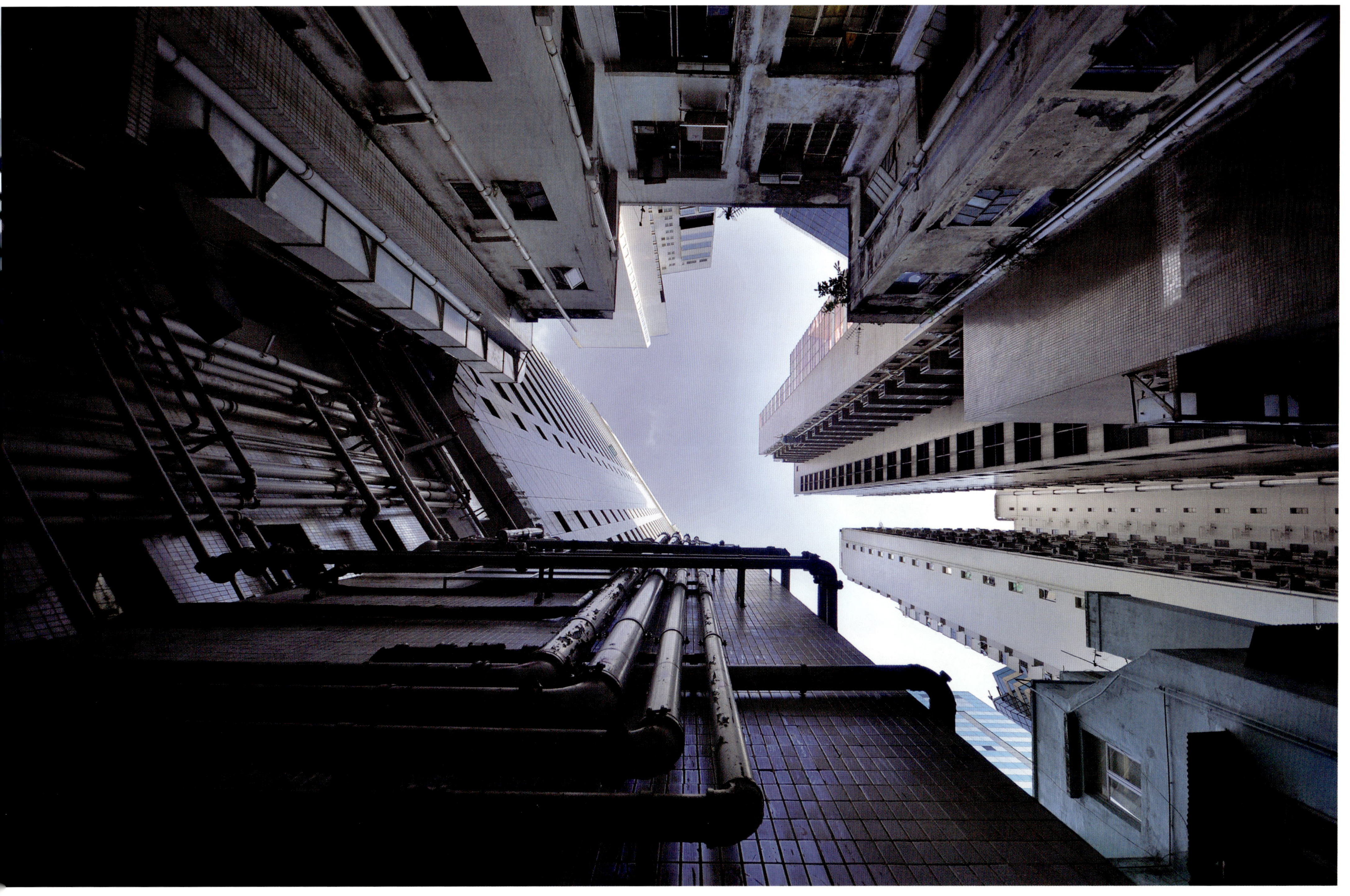

迷宮

Maze

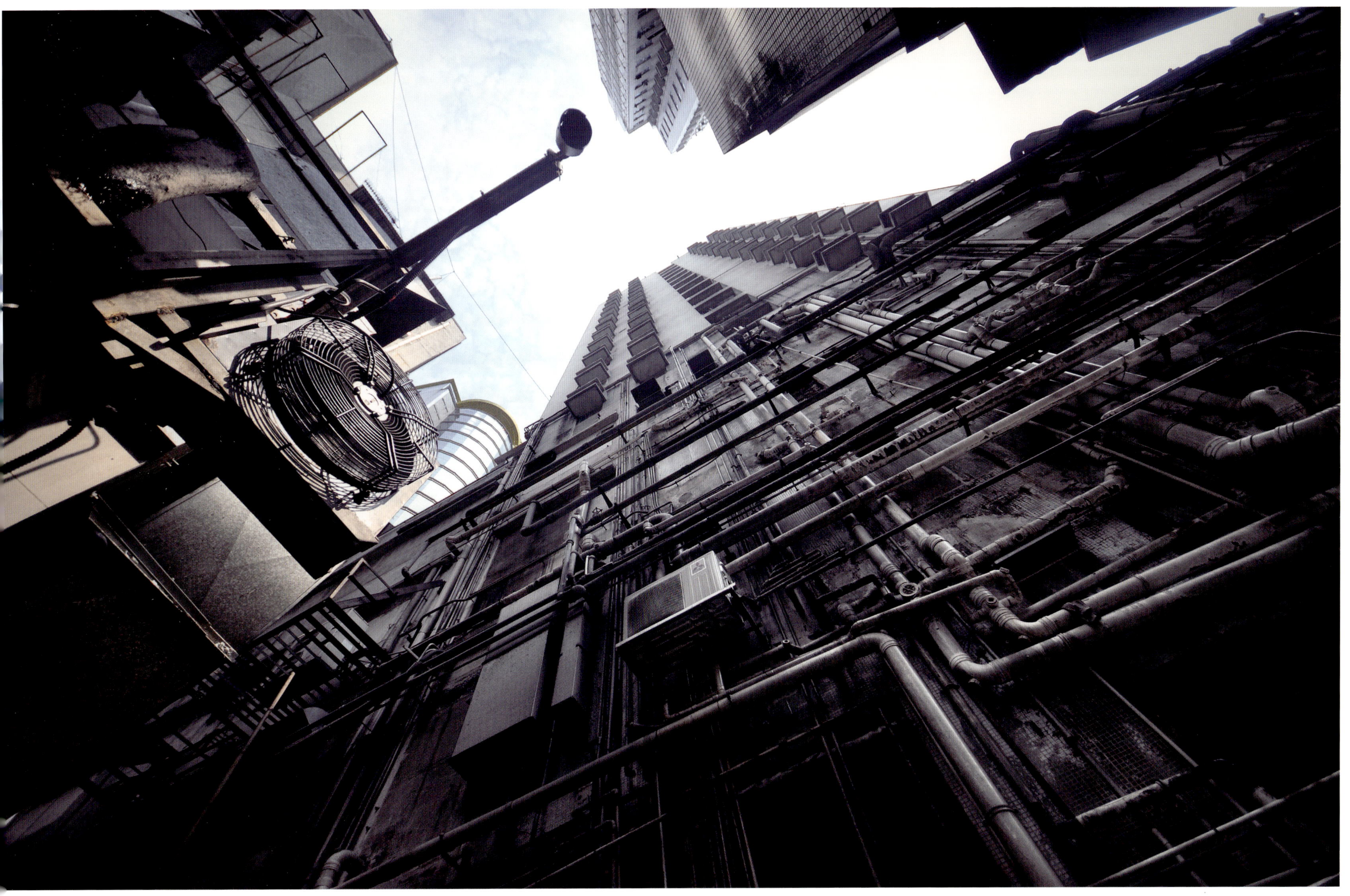

吸收

Absorption

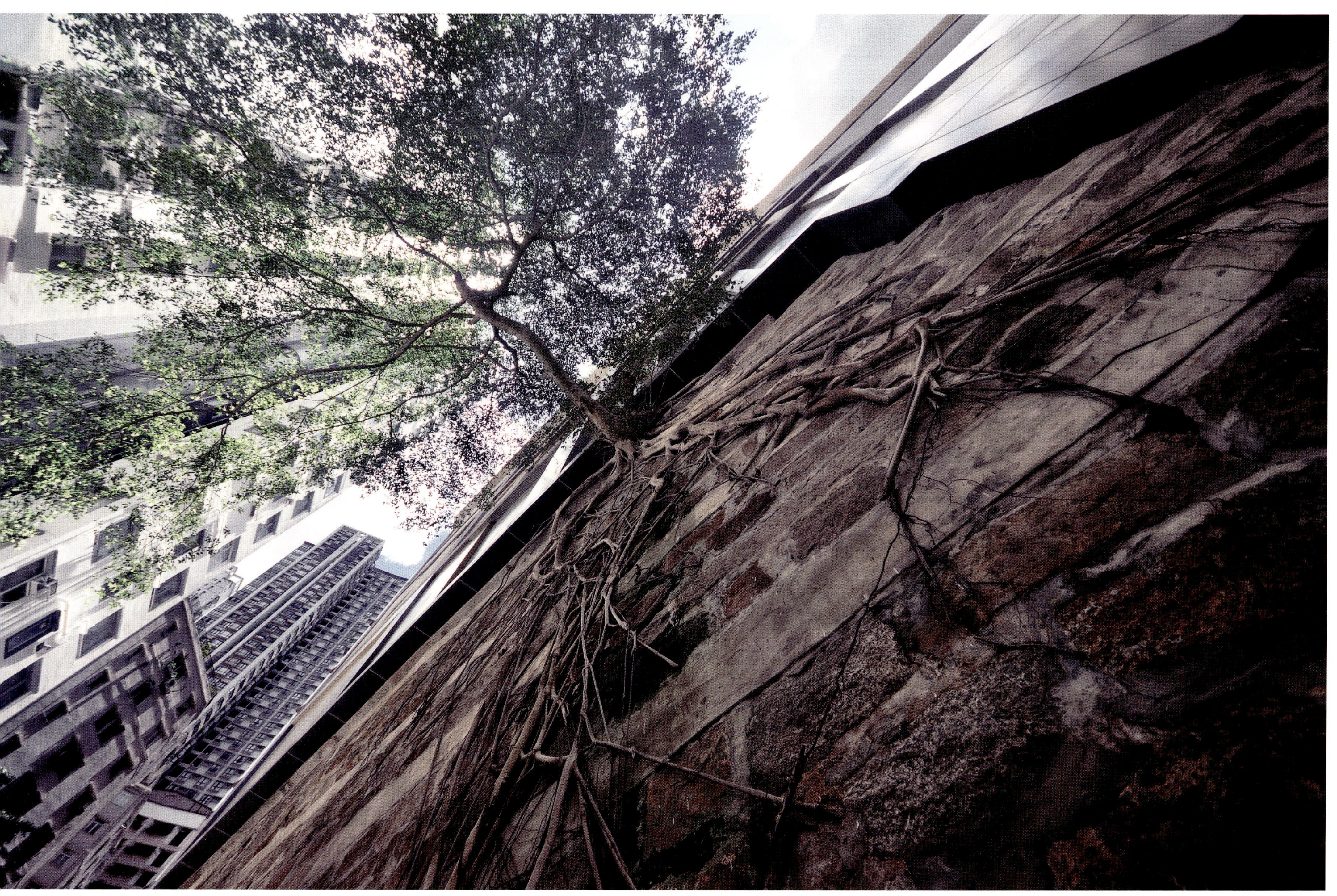

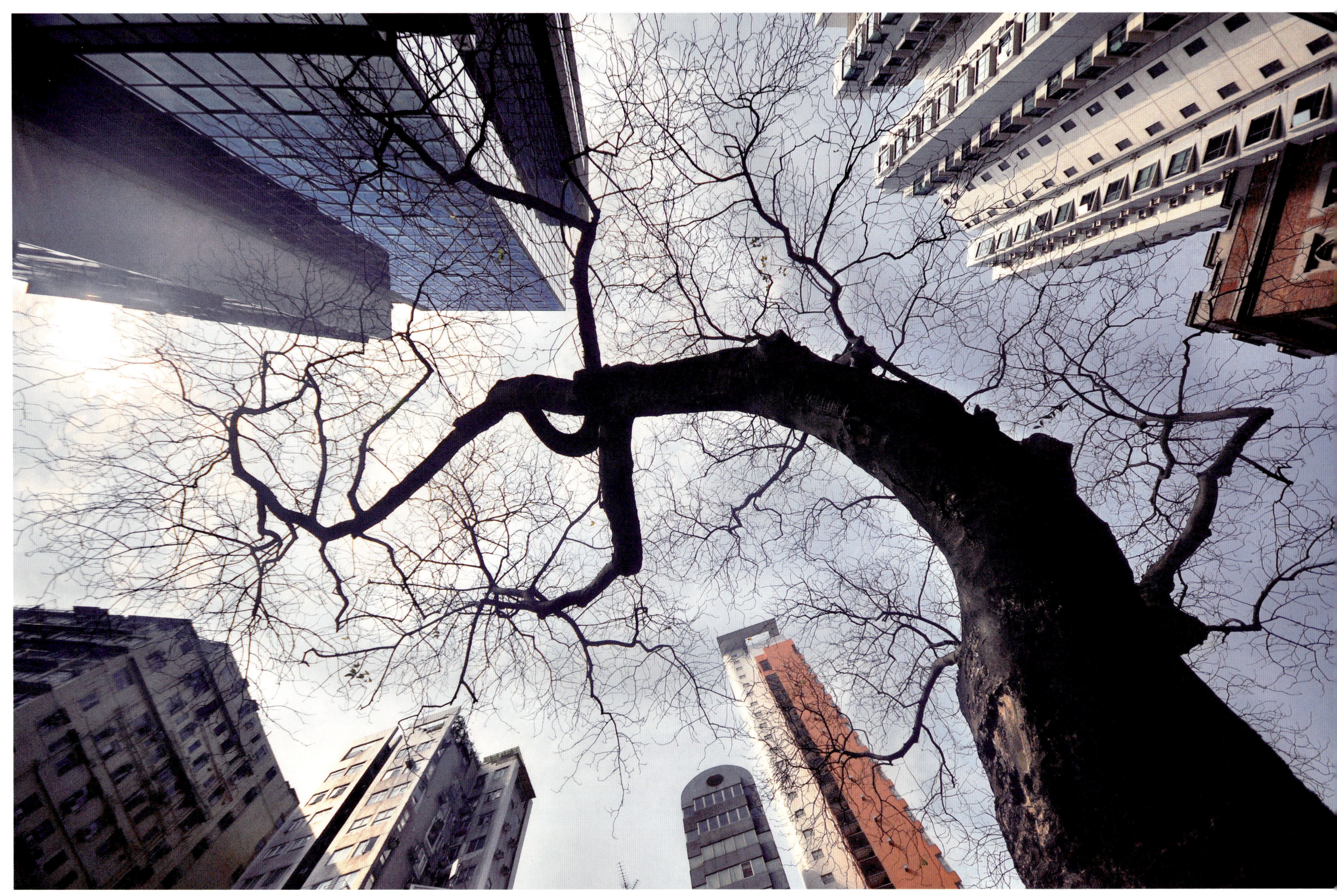

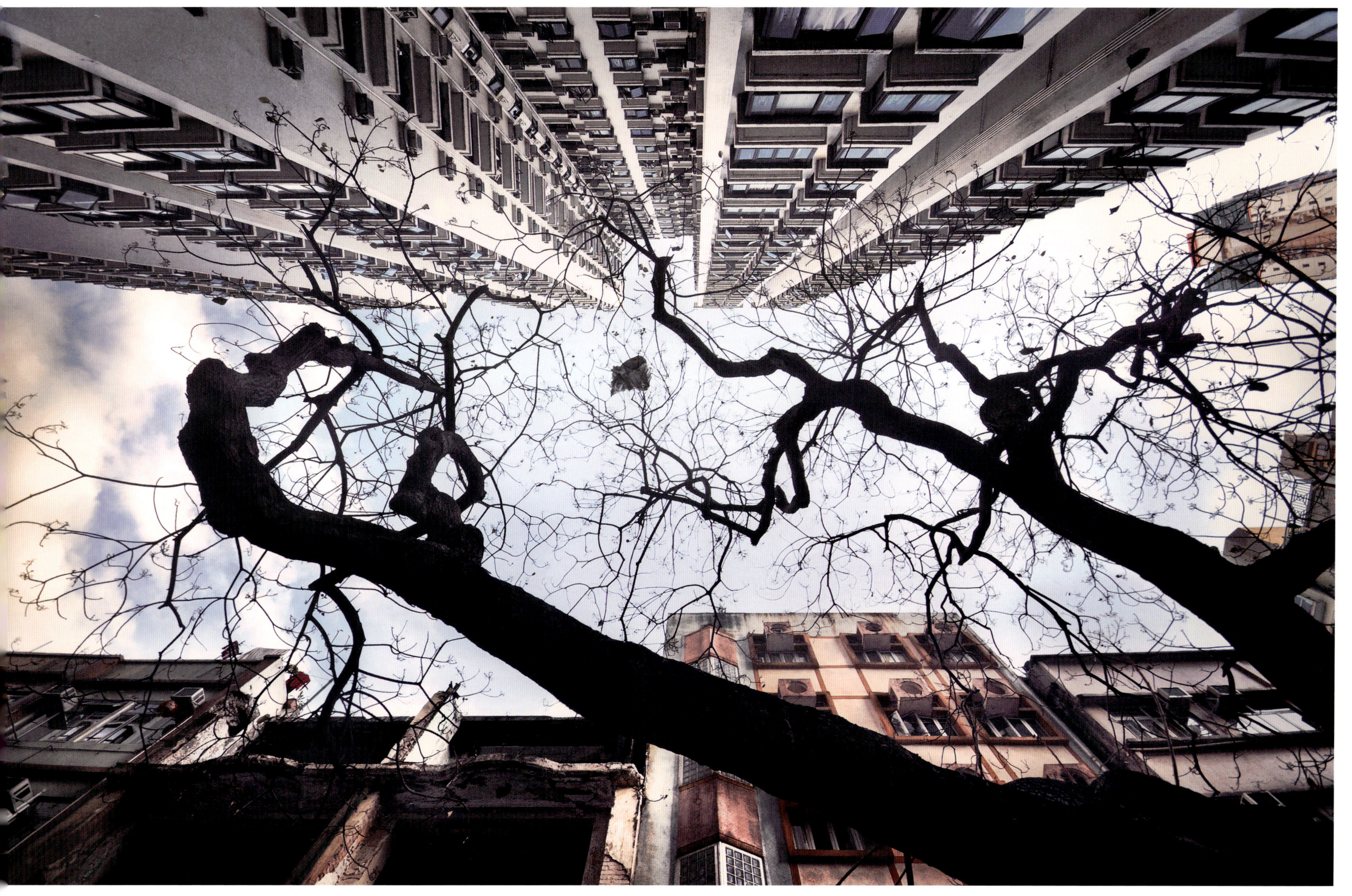

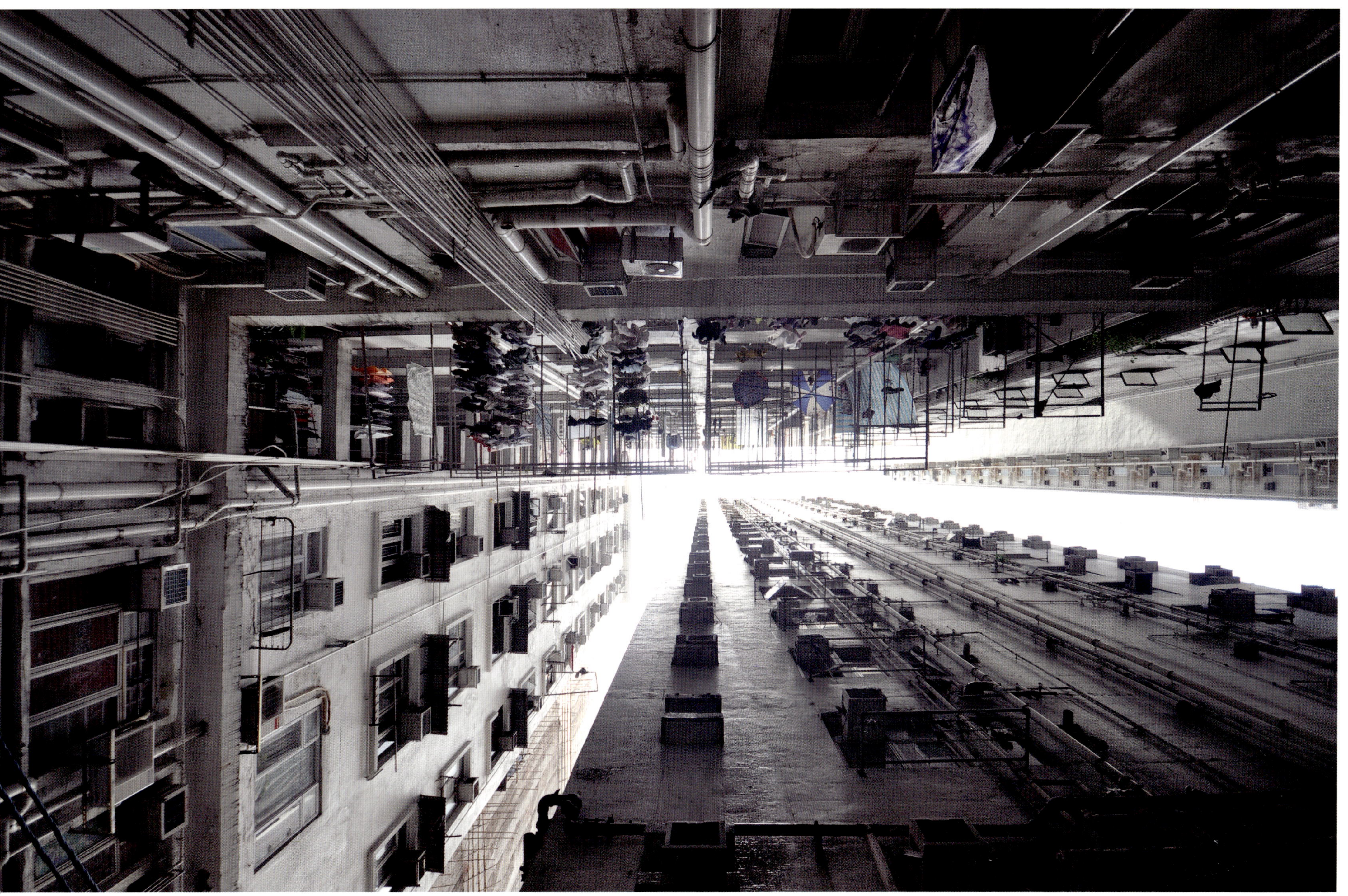

建「竹」

Bamboo Weavers

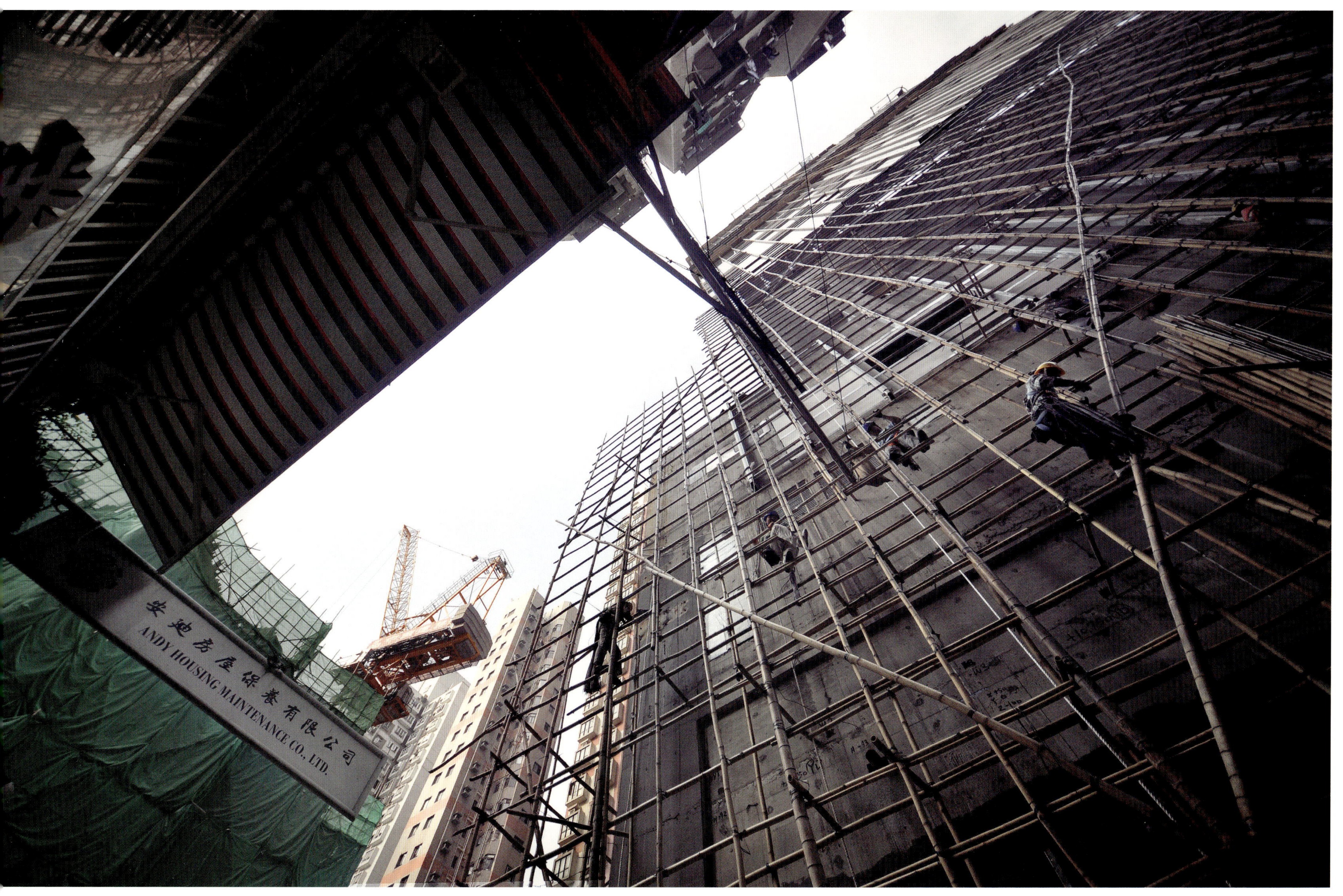
安迪房屋保養有限公司
ANDY HOUSING MAINTENANCE CO., LTD.

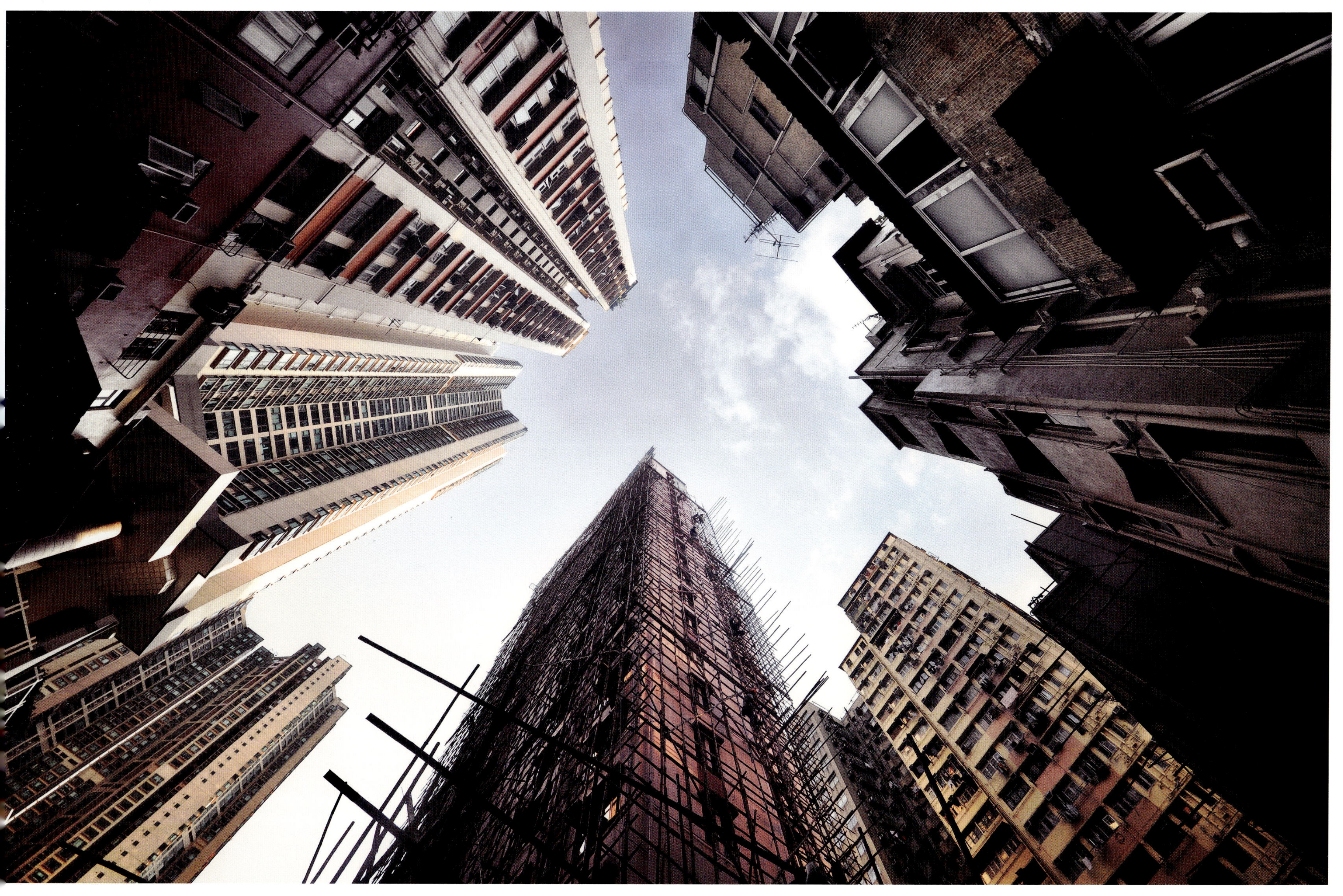

競豔

Vivid

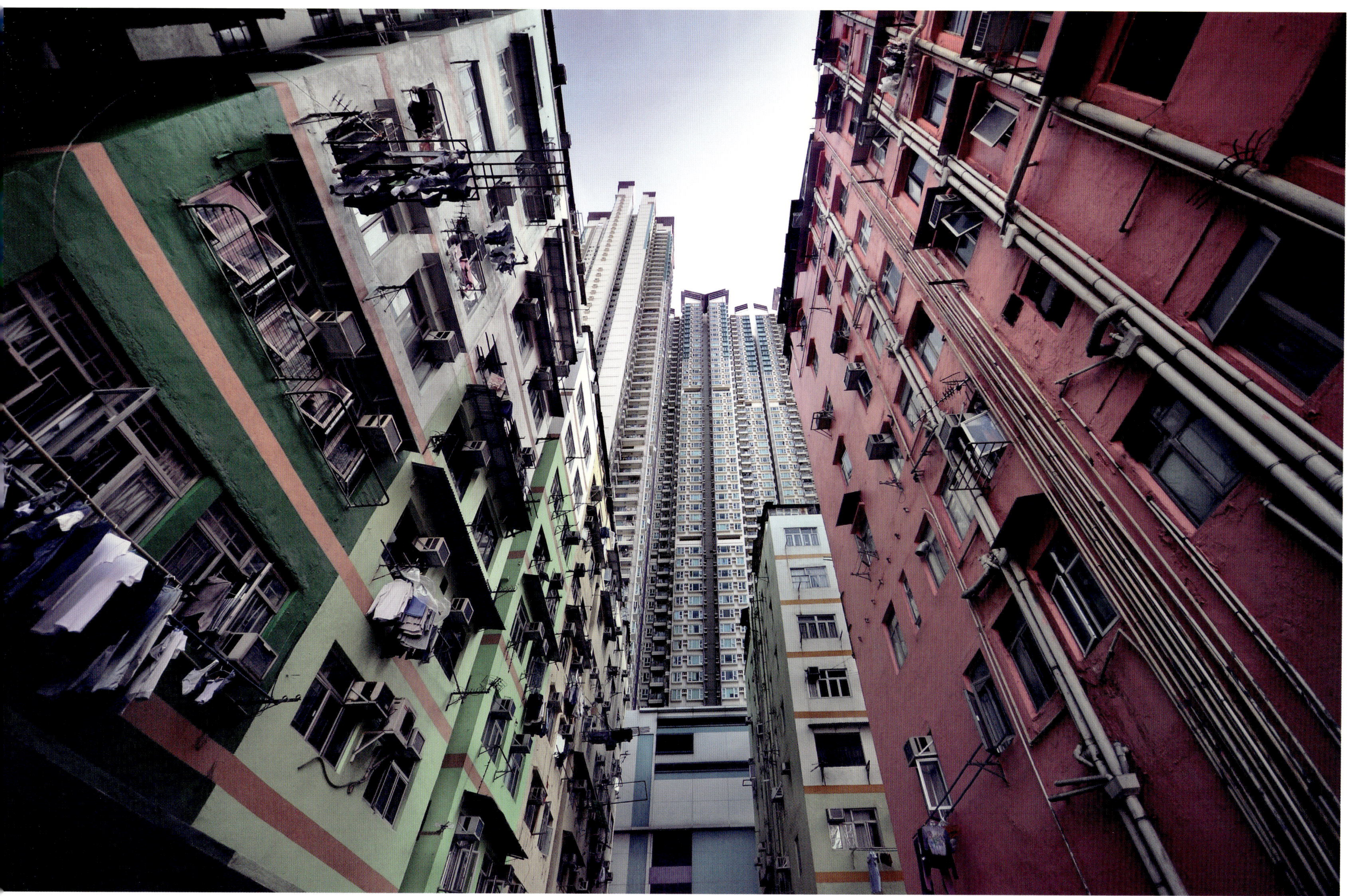

懸空

Suspend

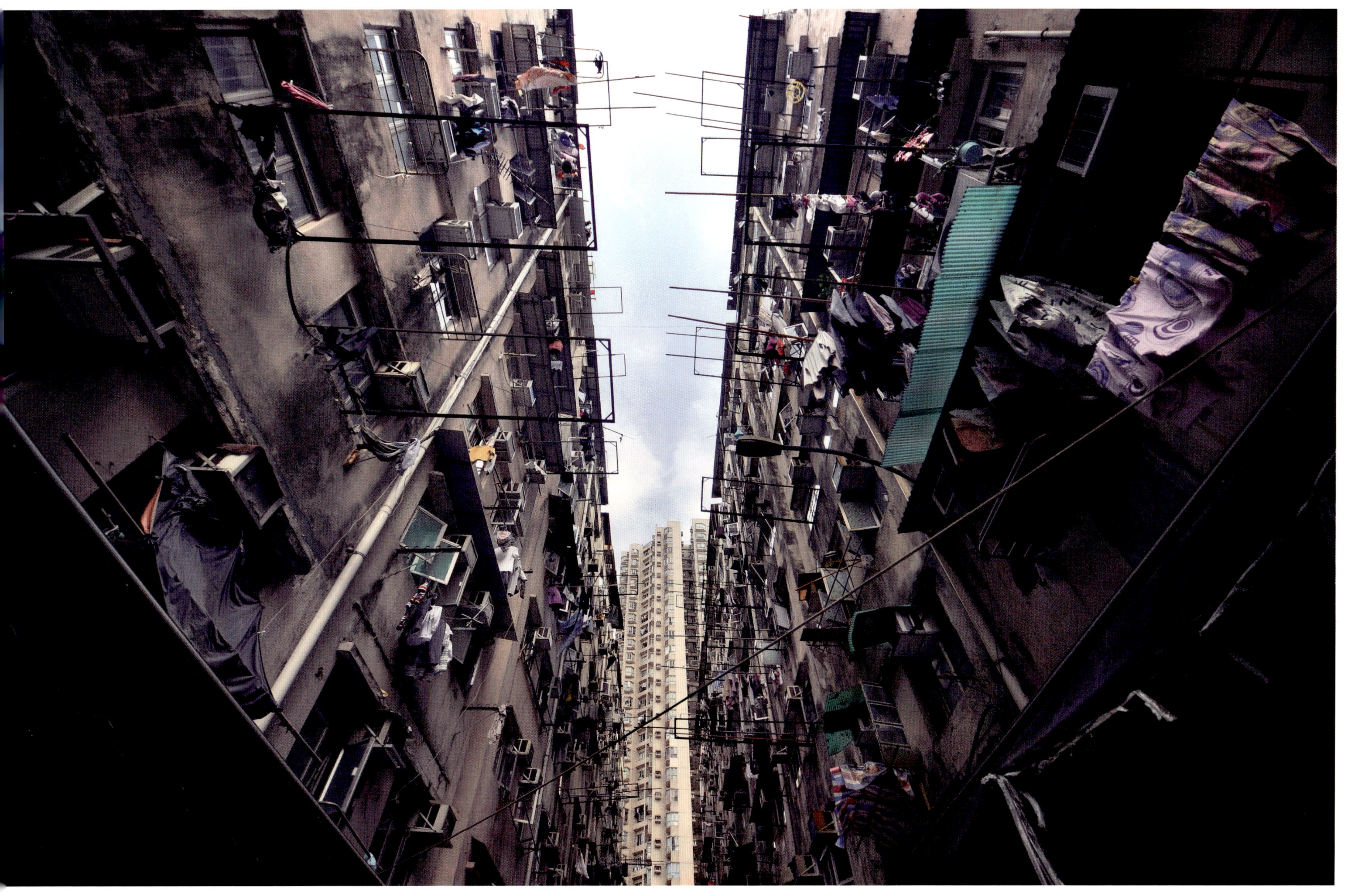

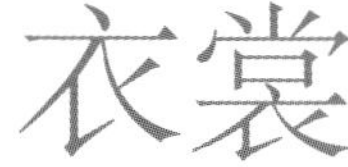

Garments

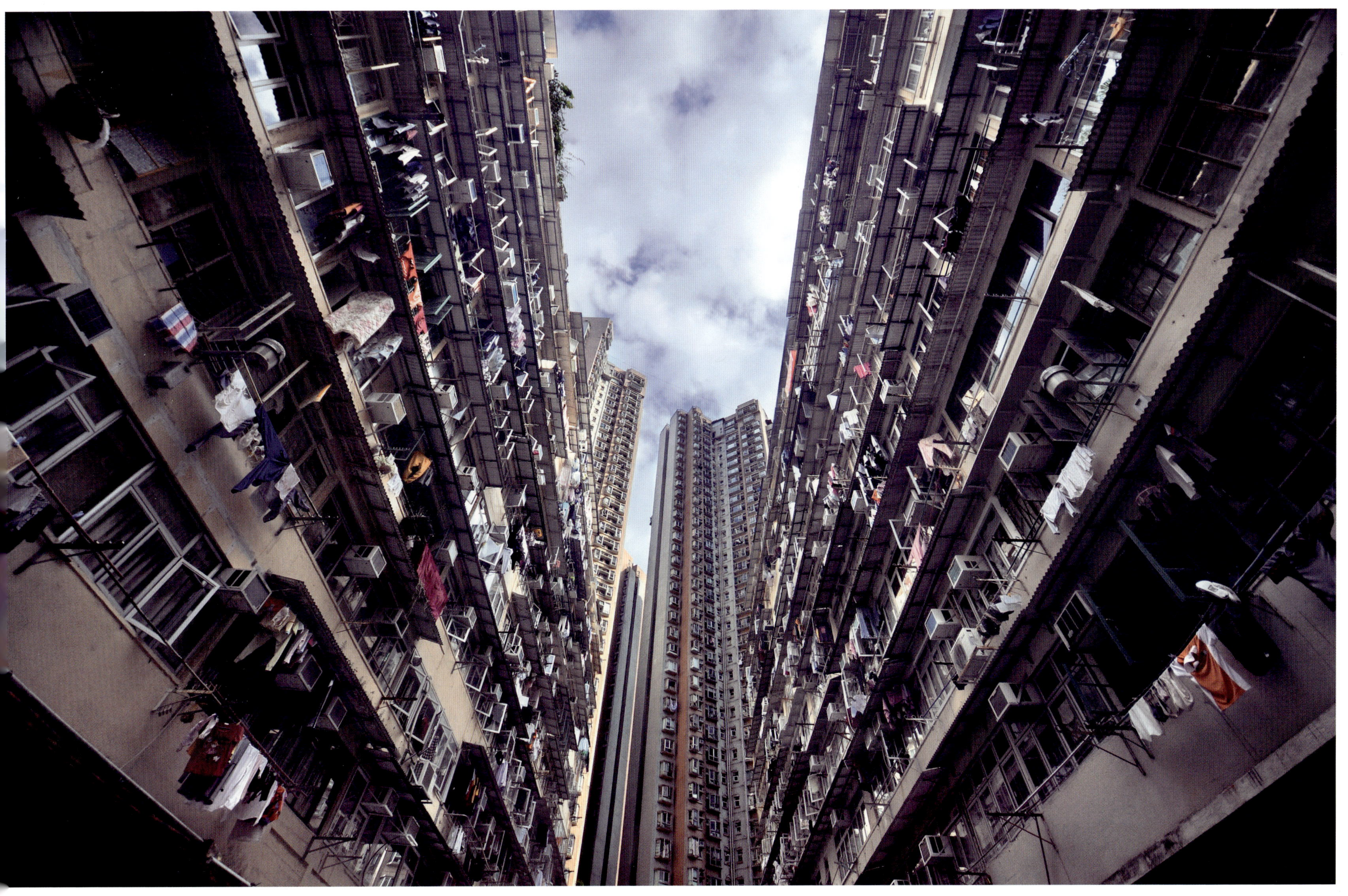

沉思

Deep Thought

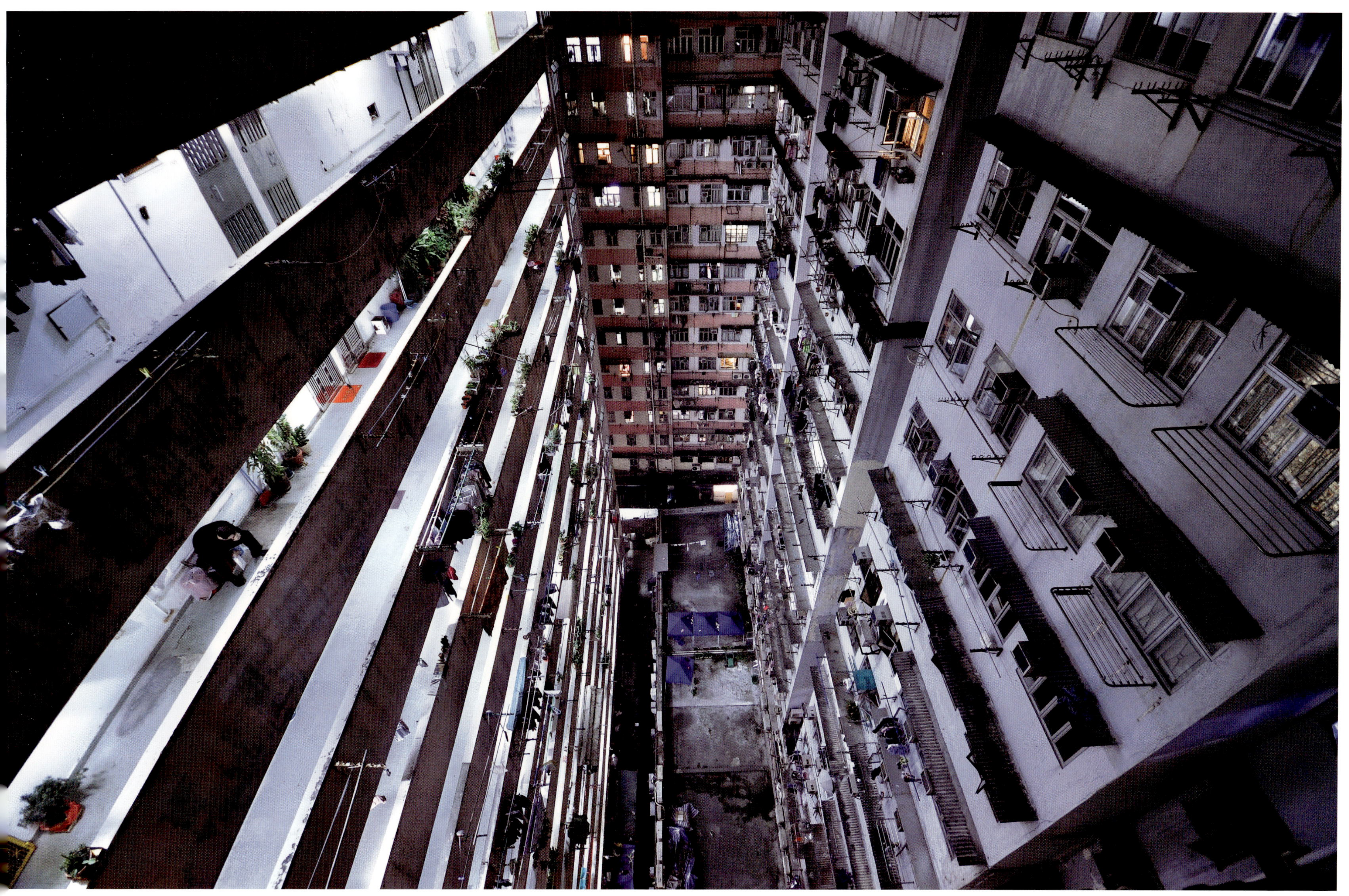

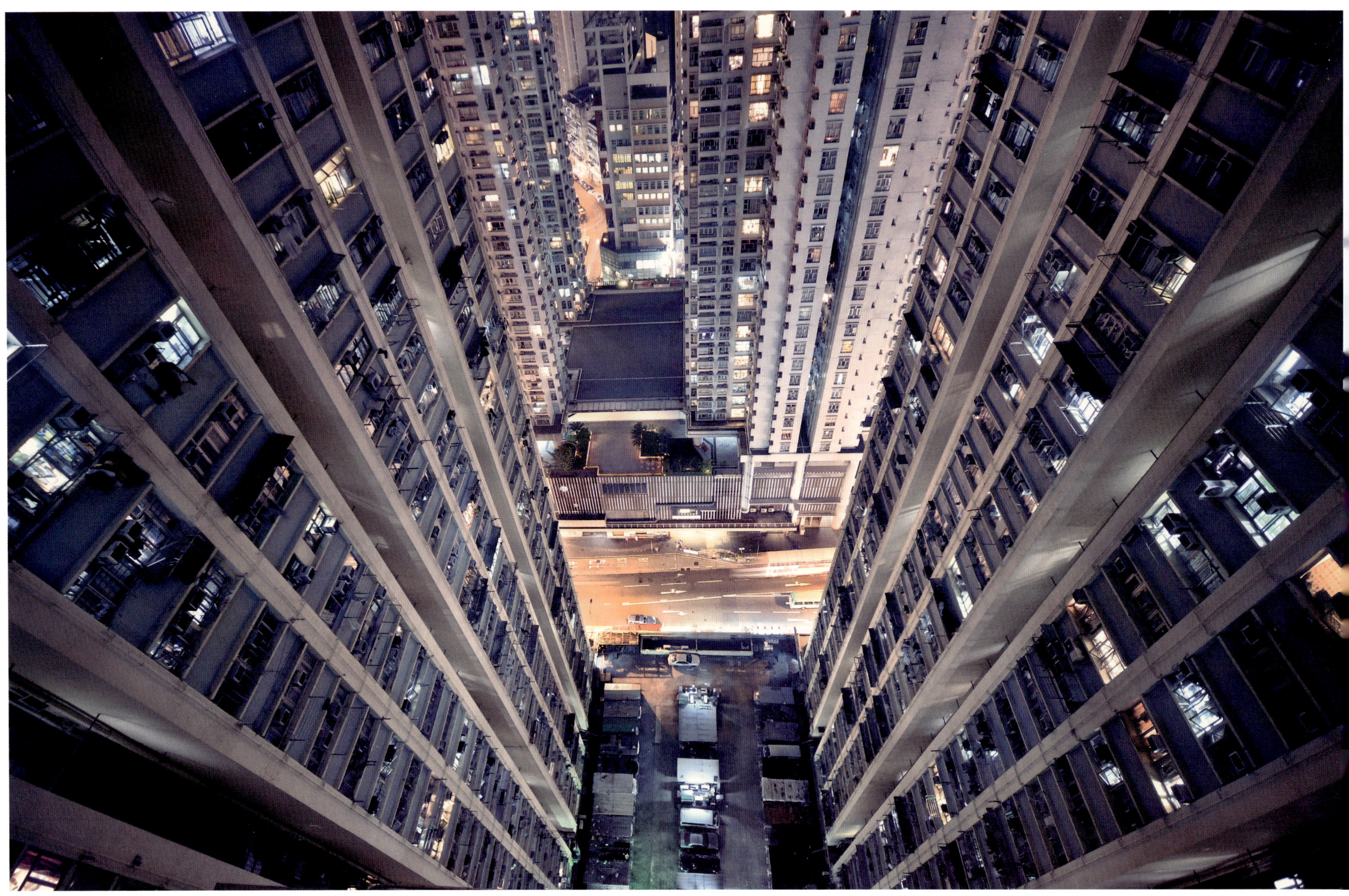

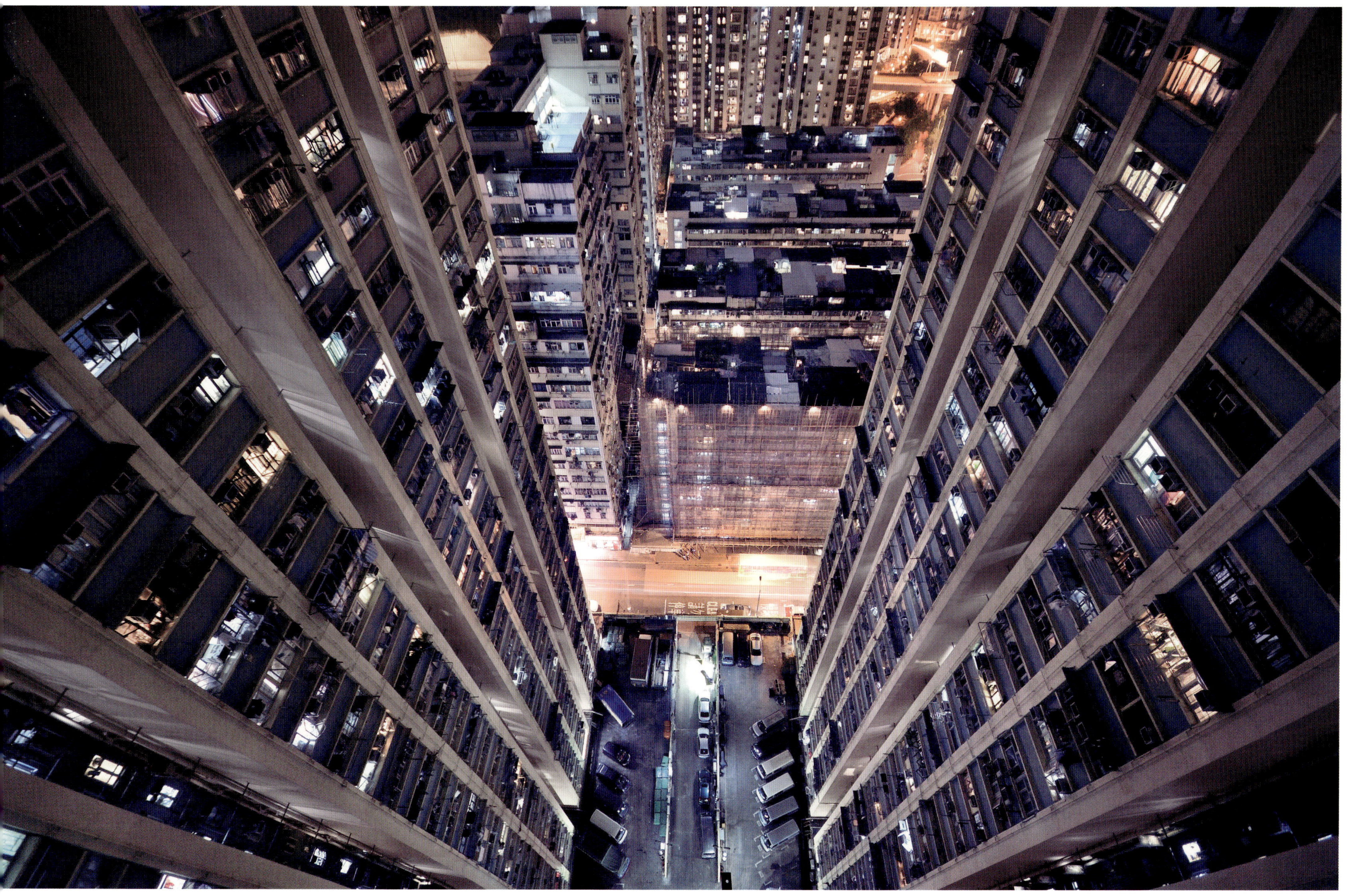

居所

Internal Life

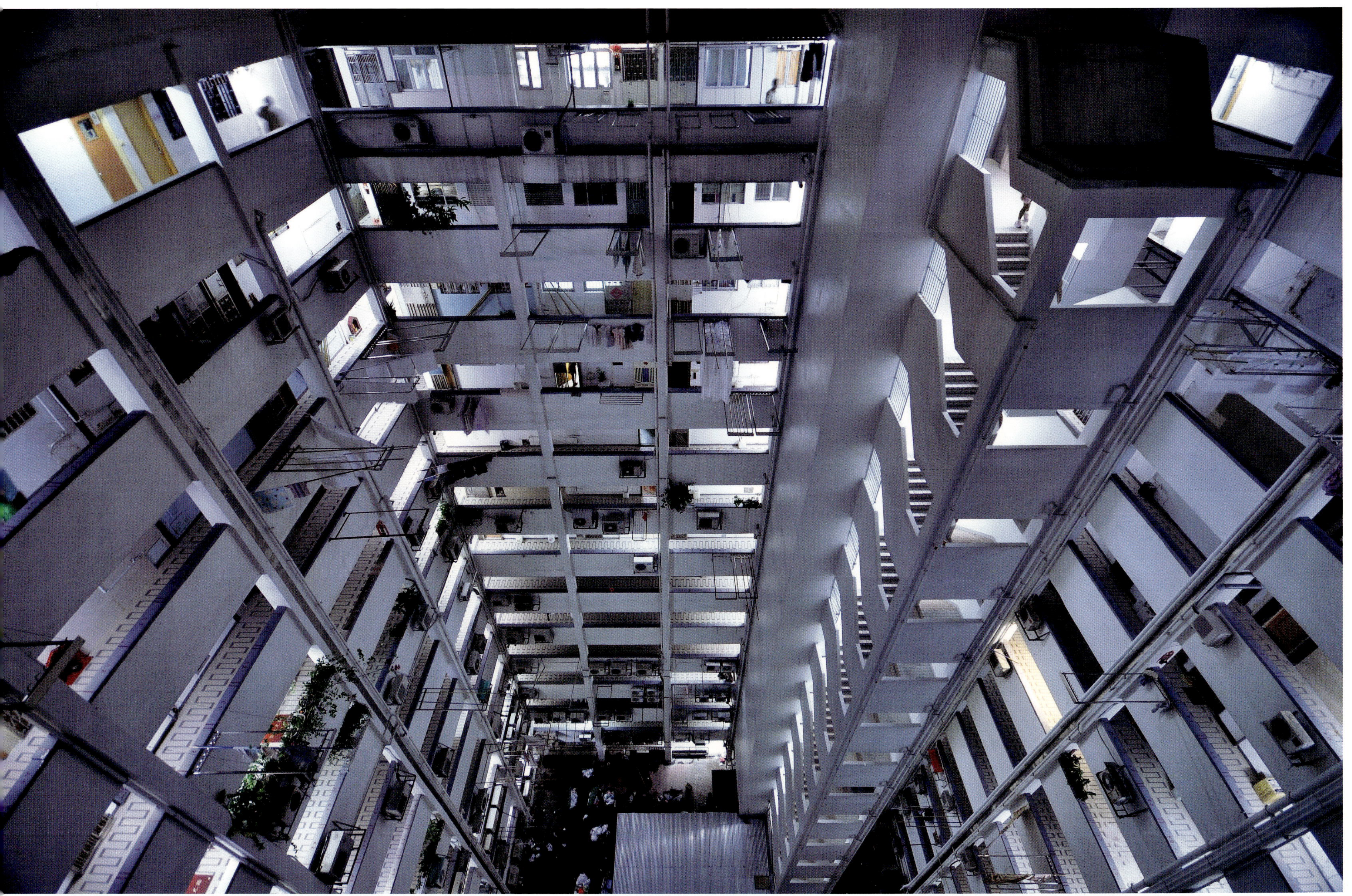

氣節

Upright

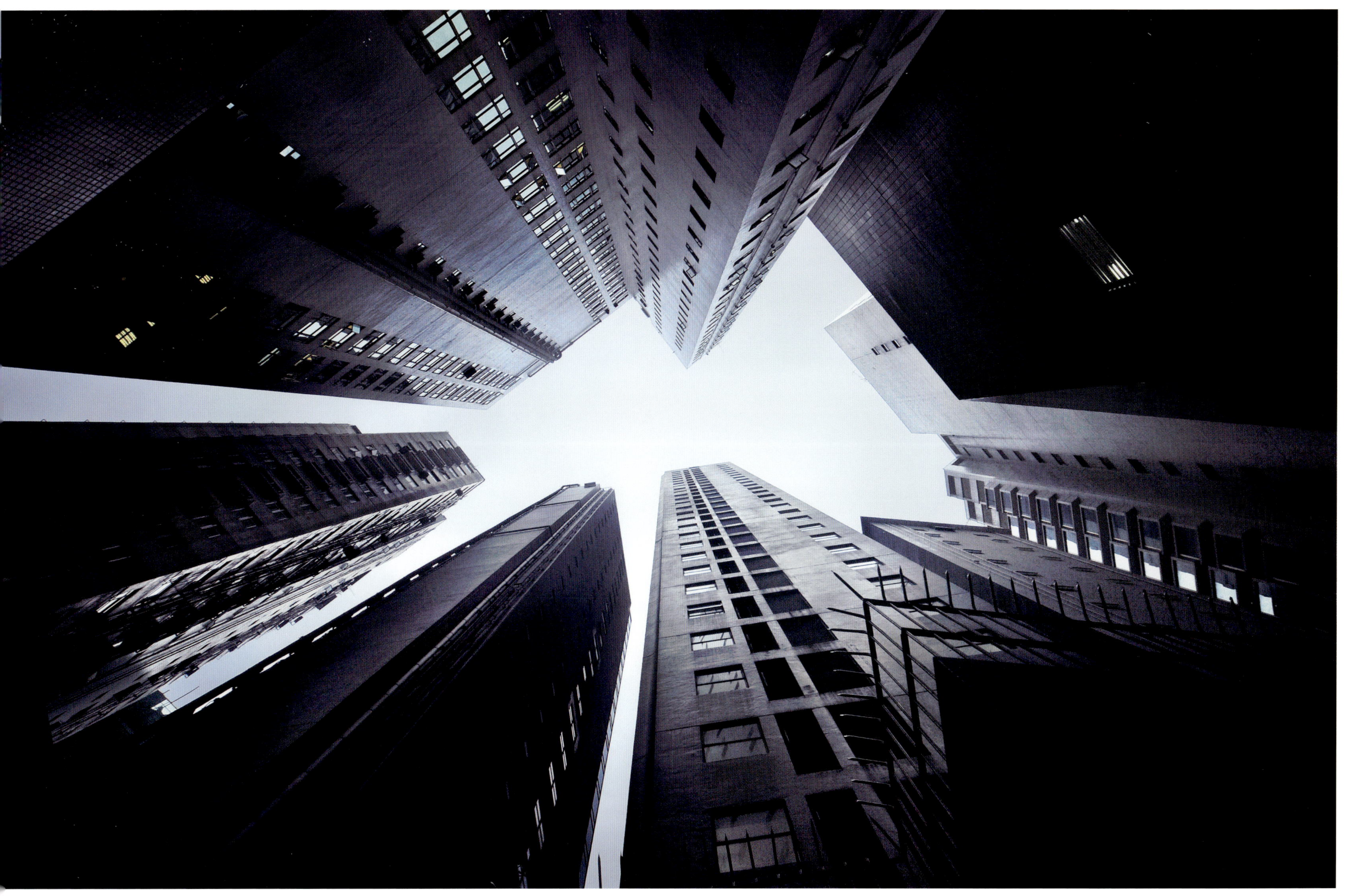

孤芳自賞

Narcissist

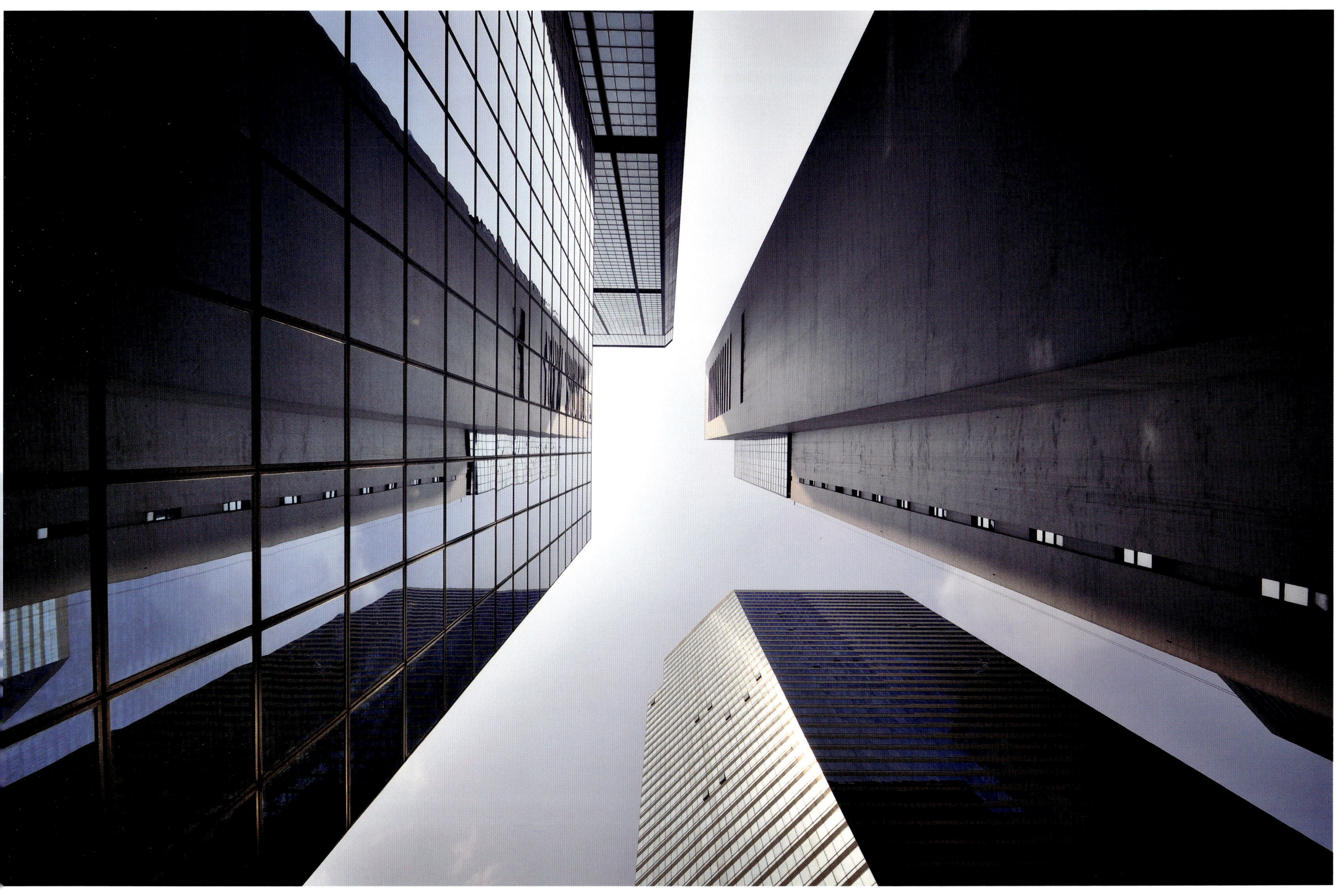

漣漪

Ripple

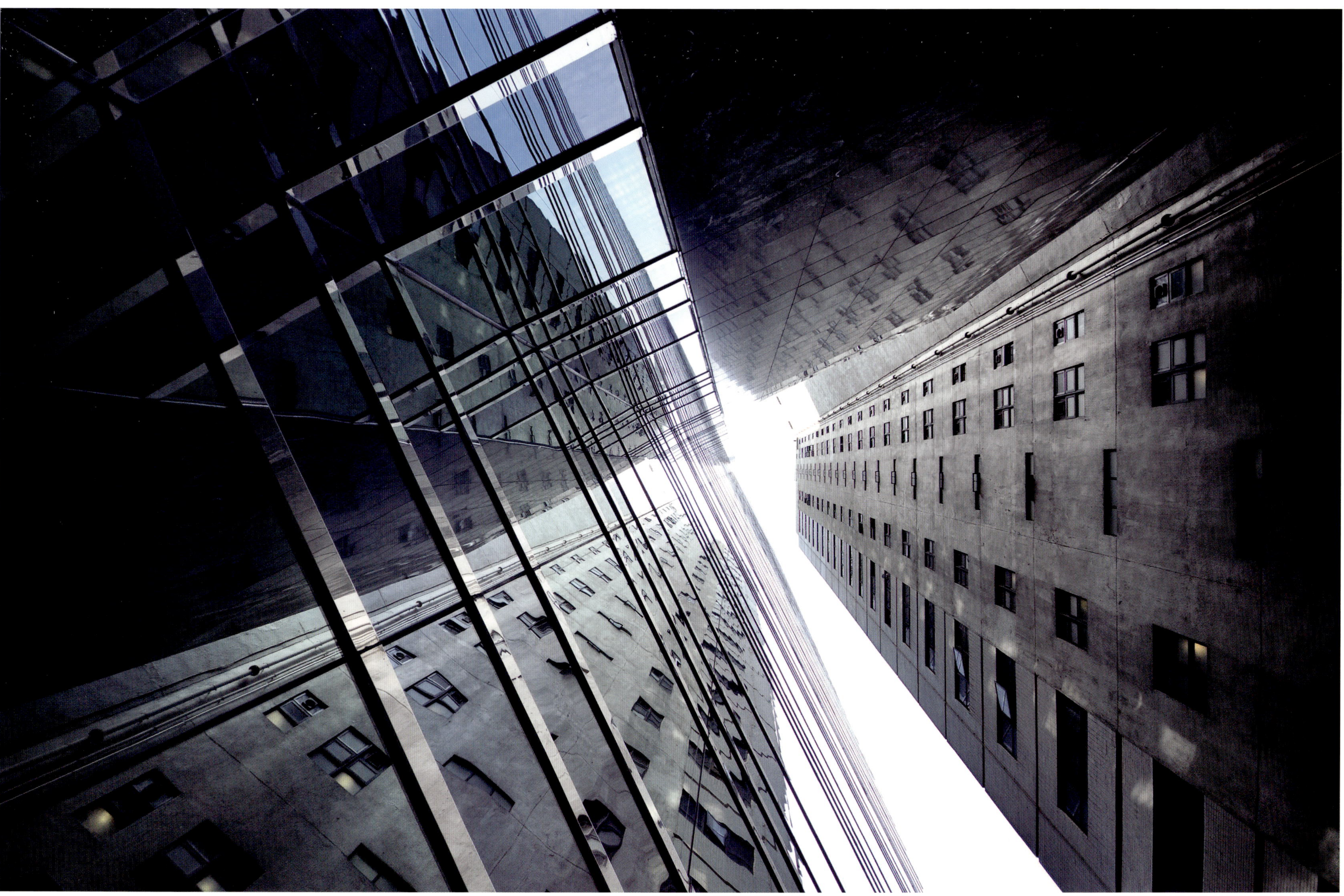

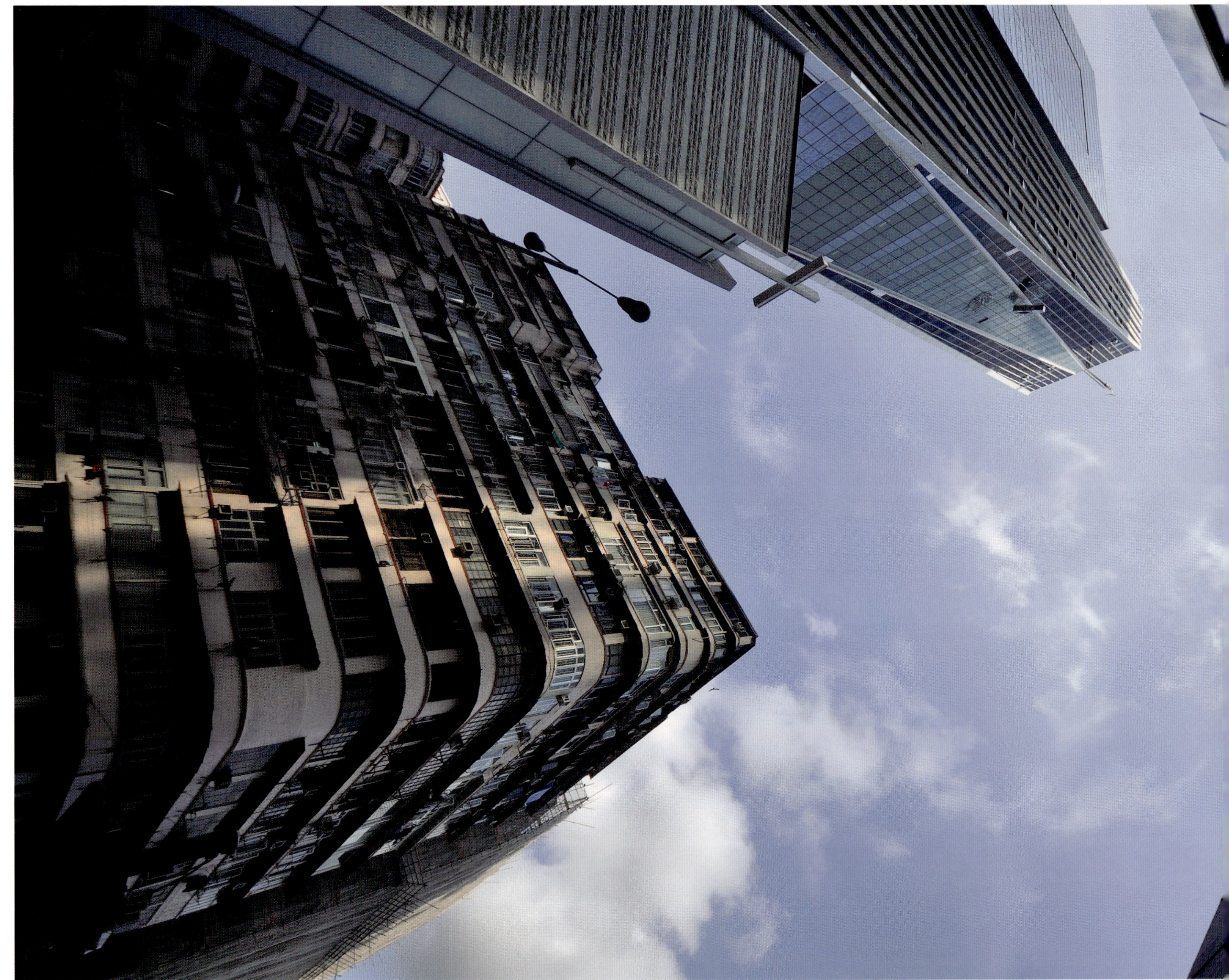

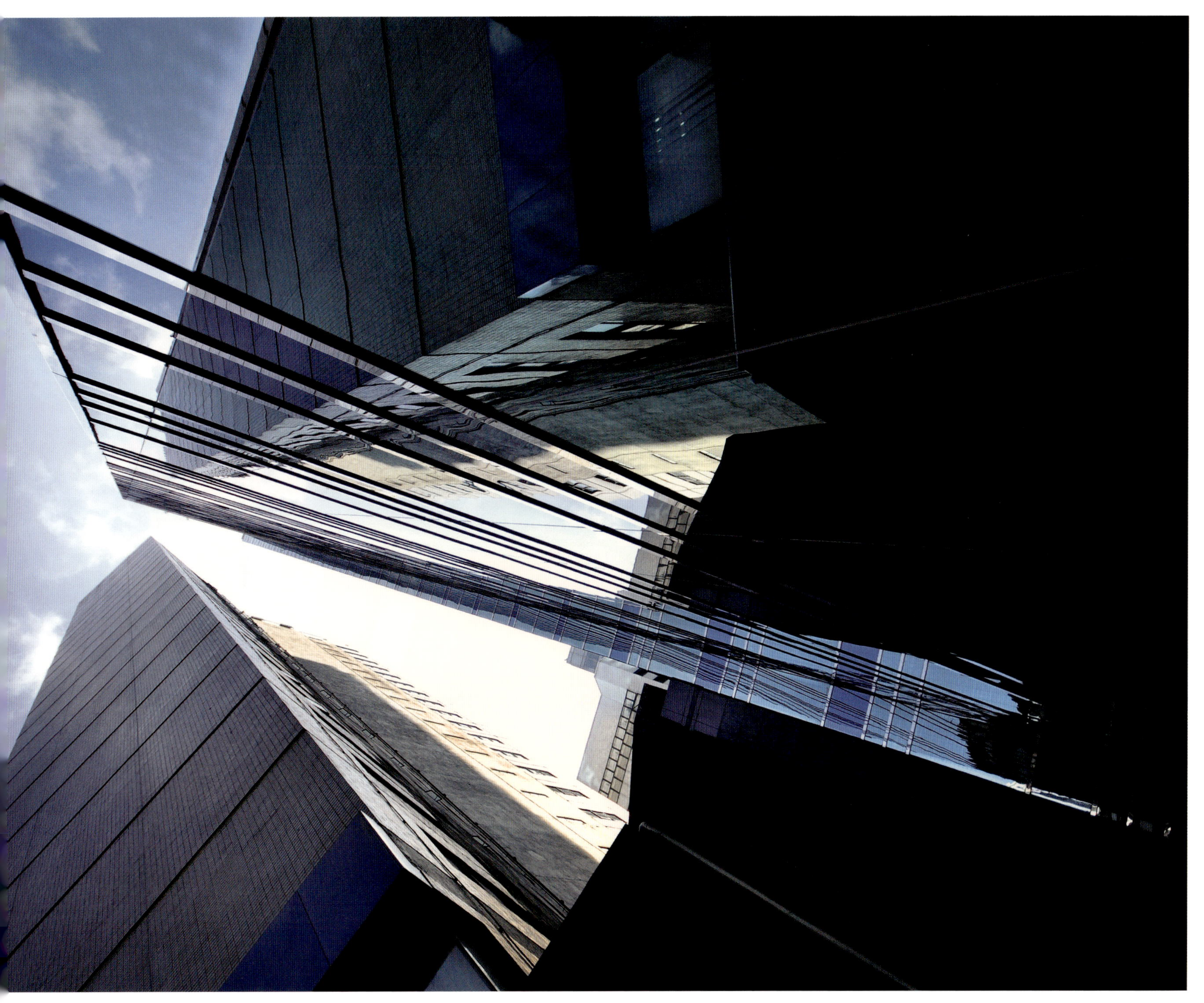

晴空

Shine

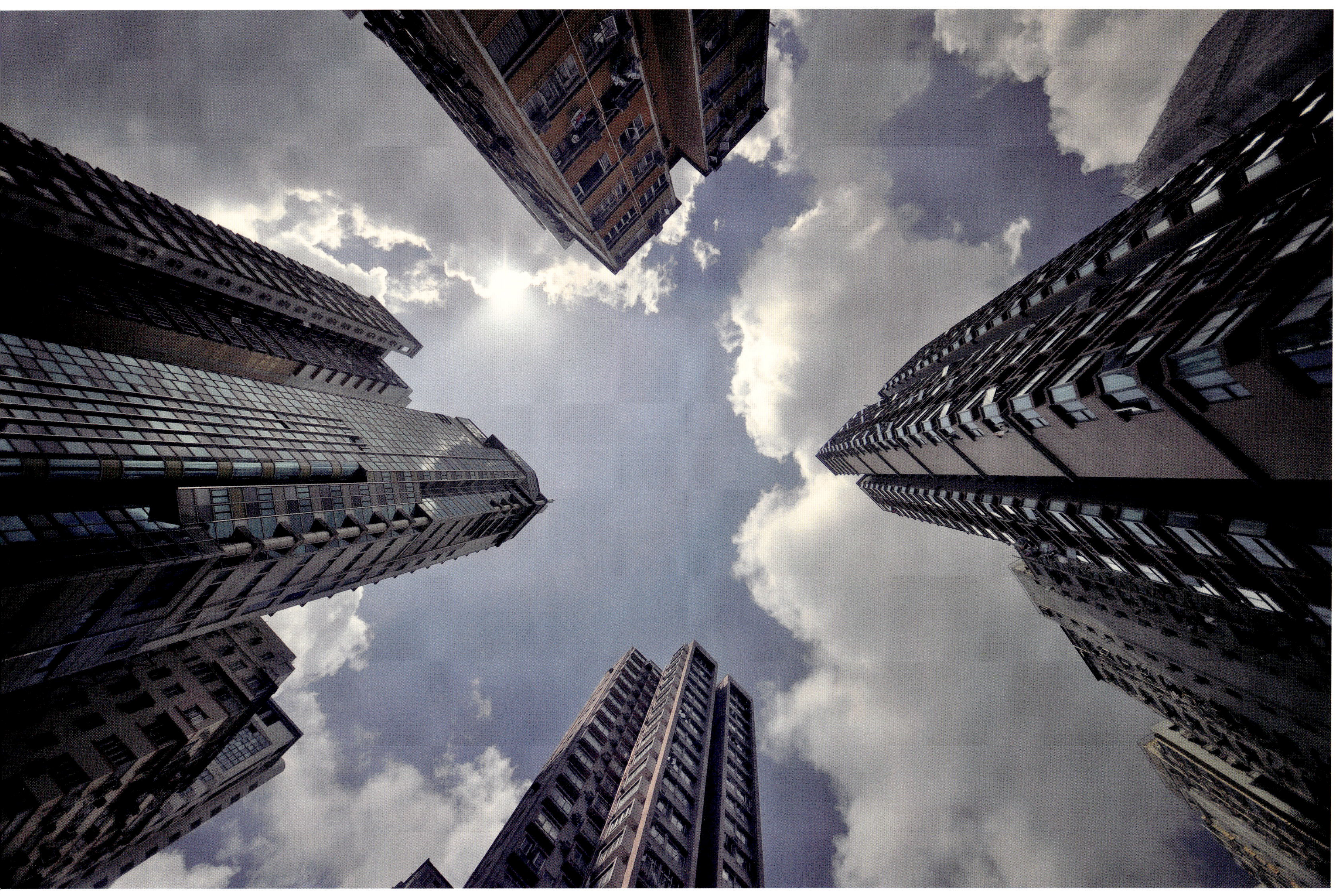

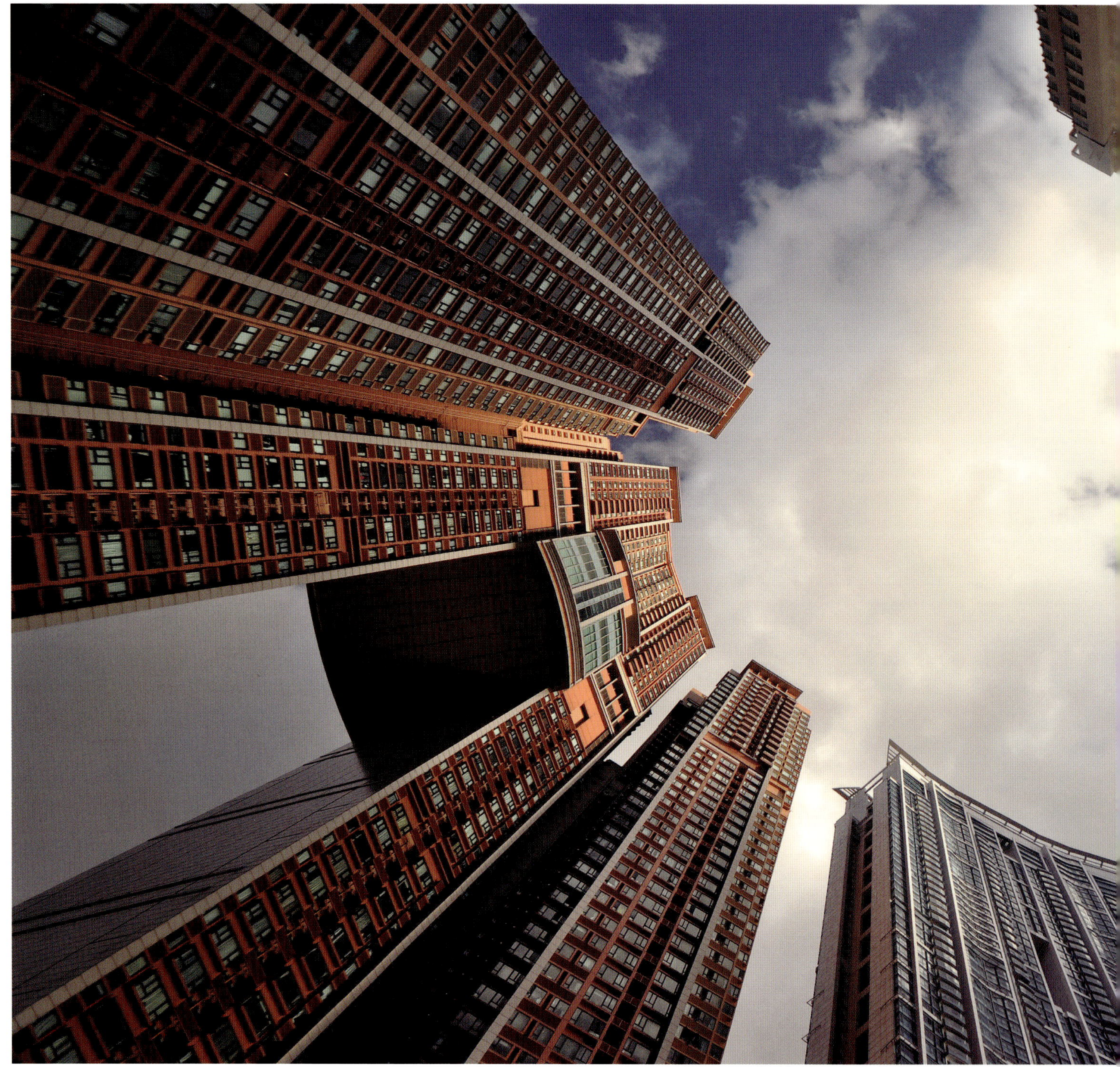

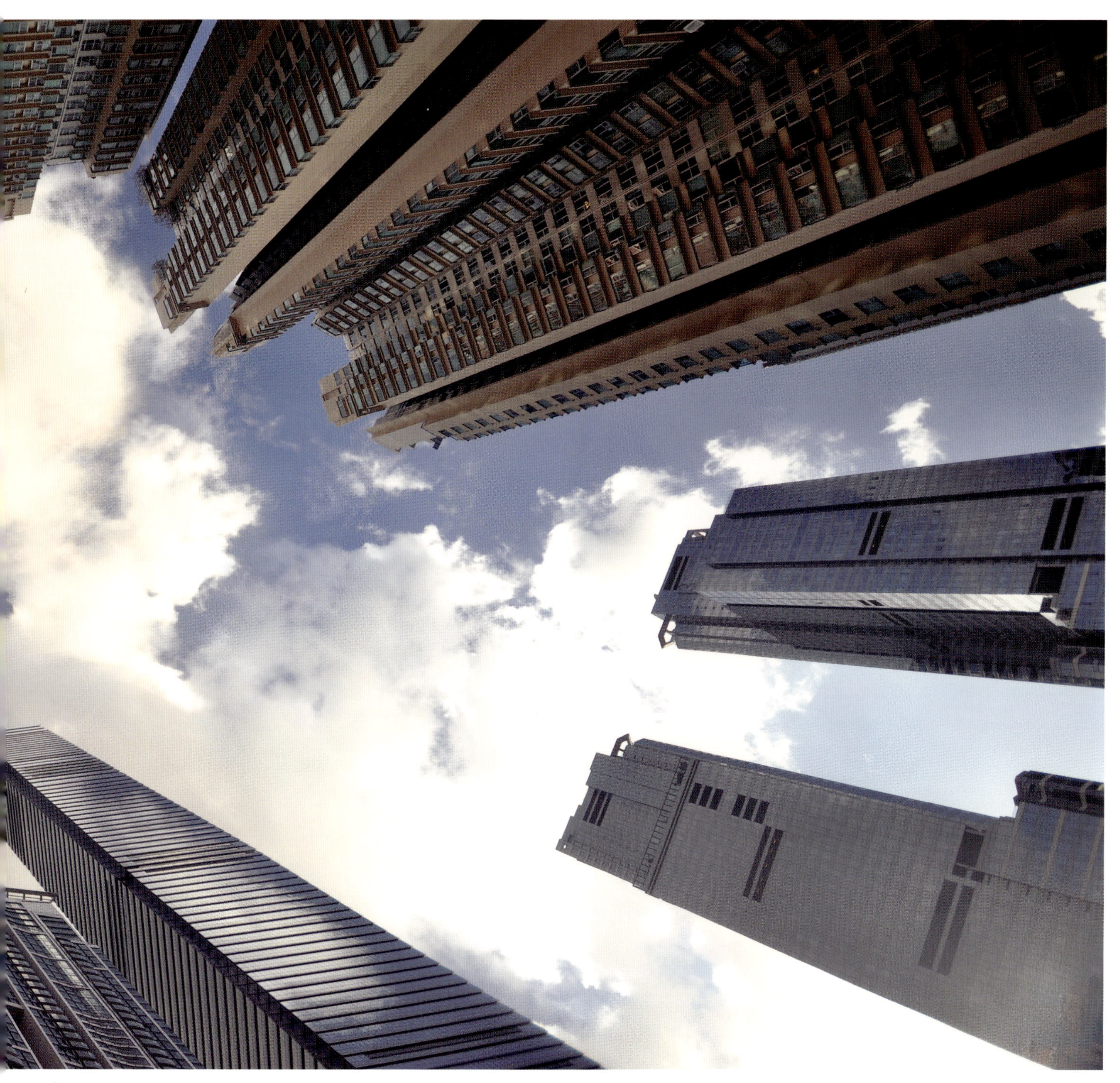

屏風

Screen

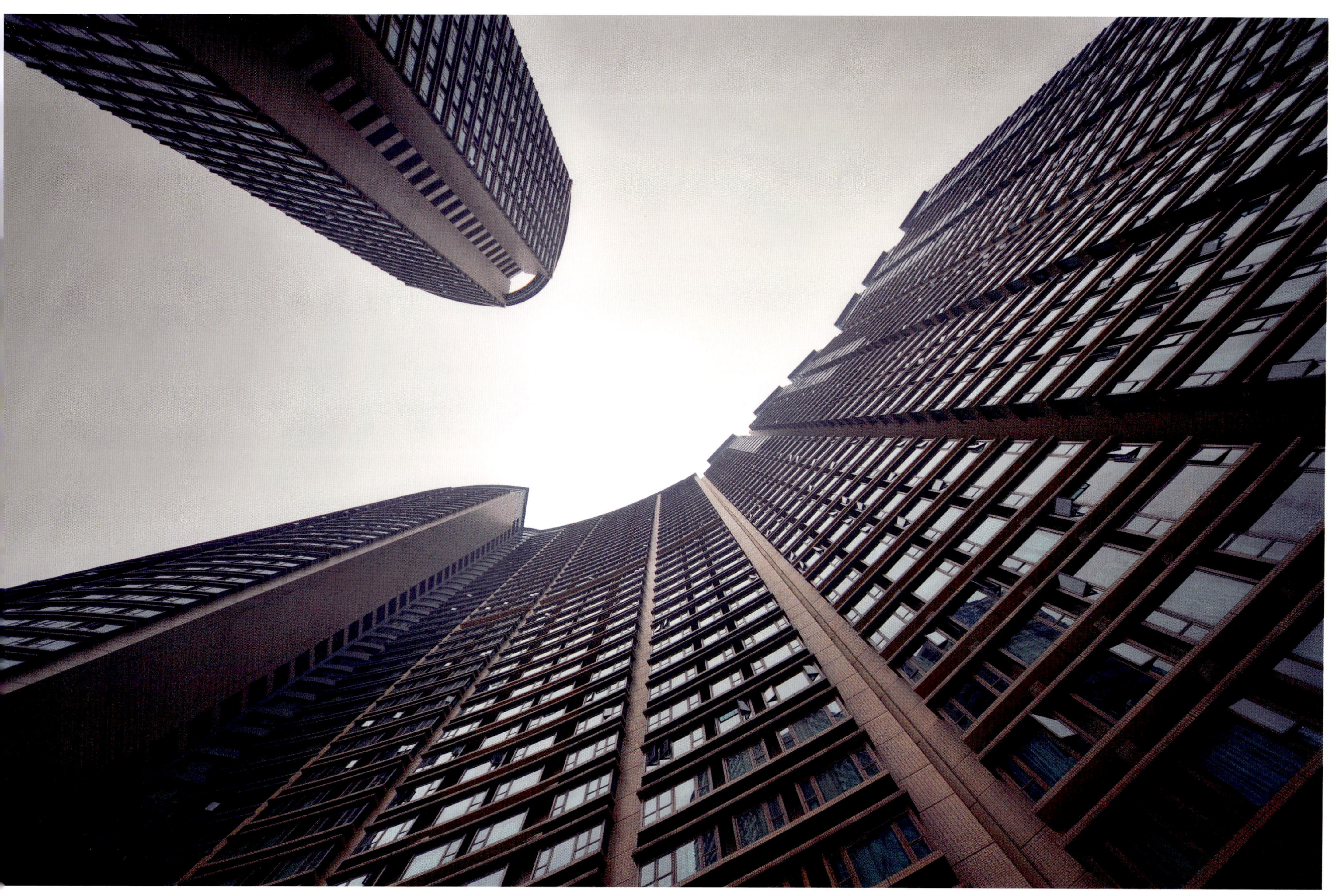

眩暈

Vertigo

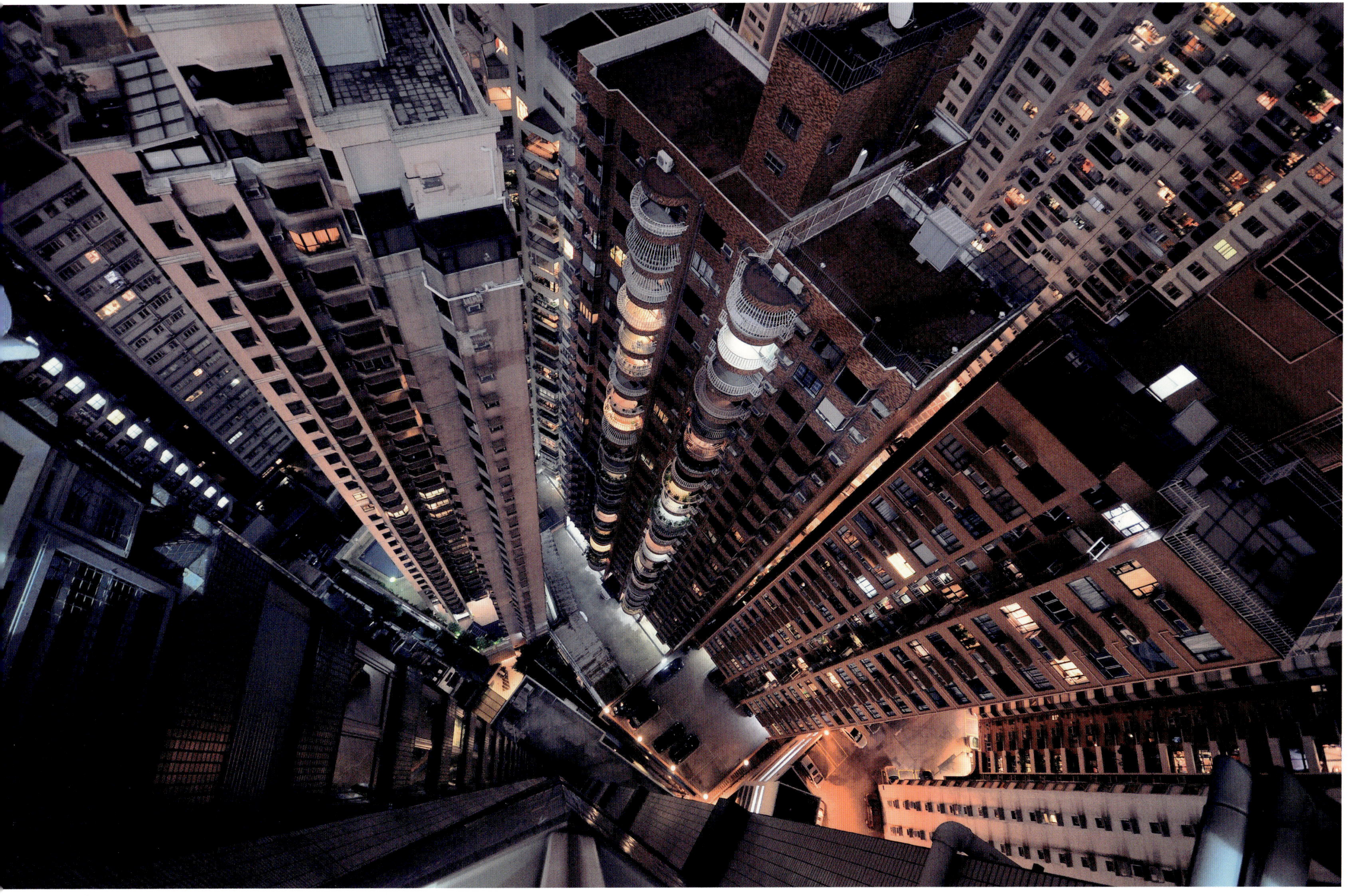

熙攘
Bustling

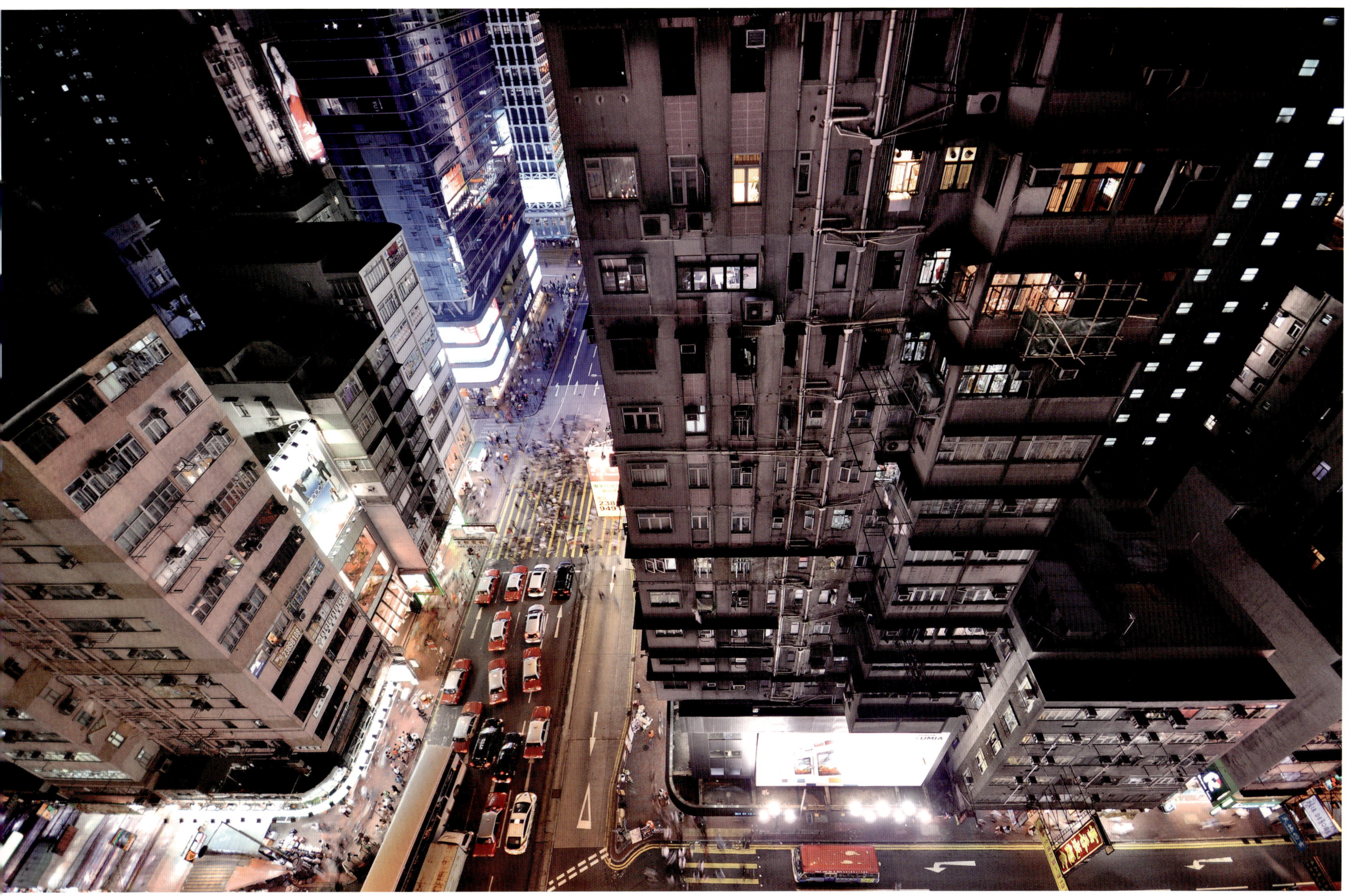

夕陽

Dusk

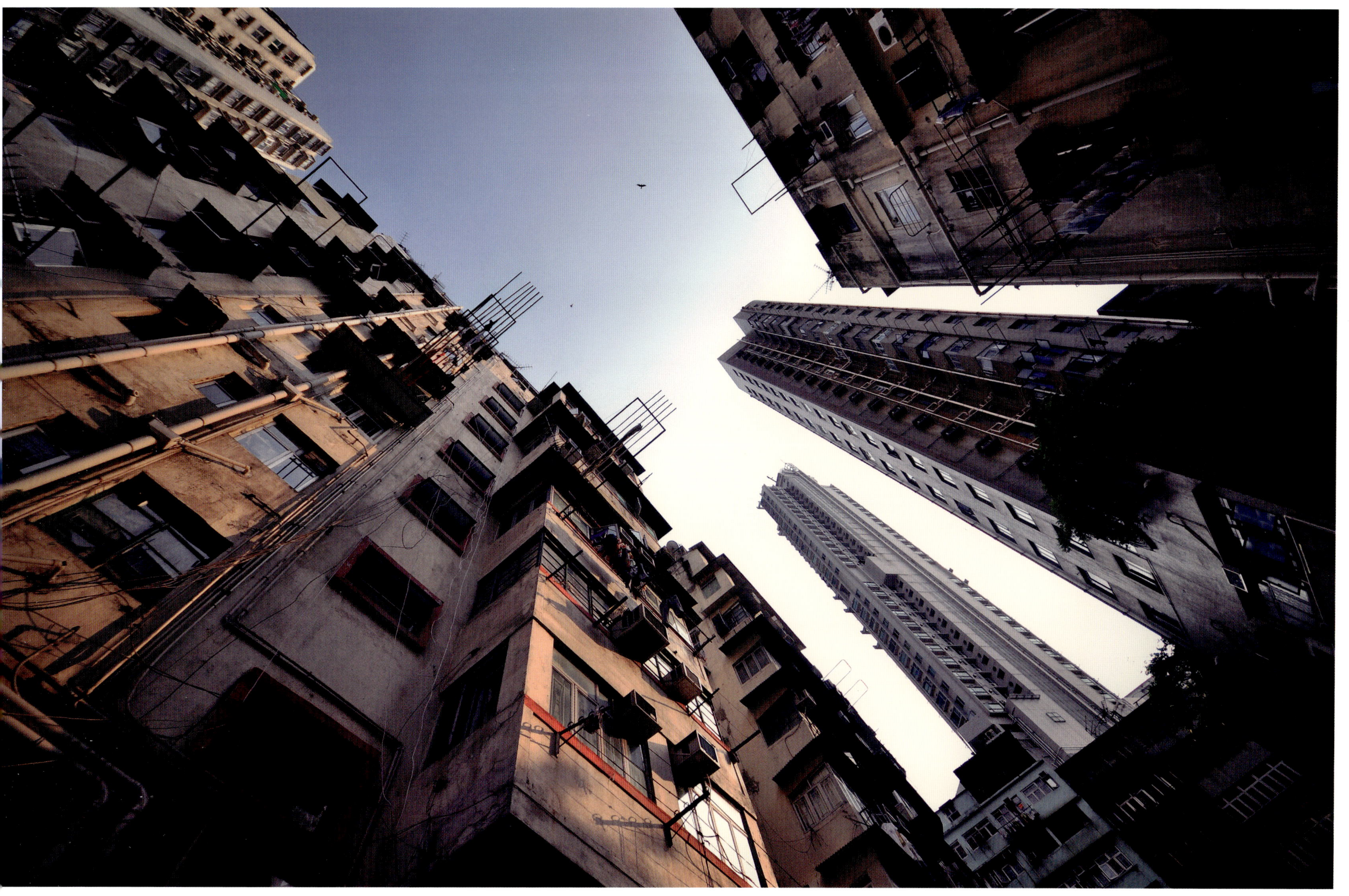

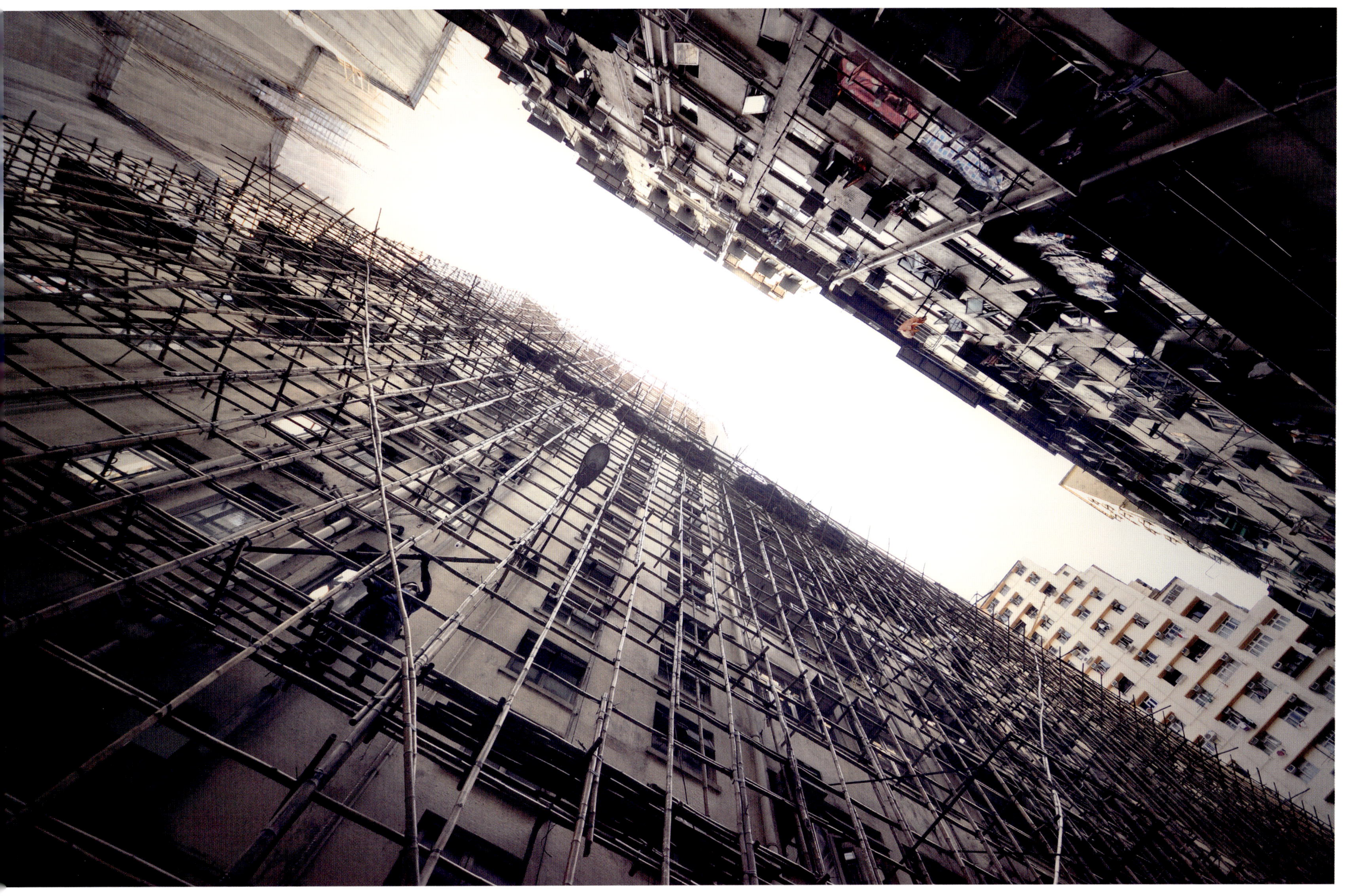

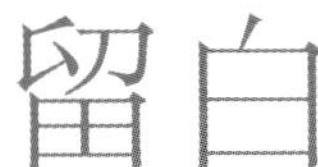

Missing piece

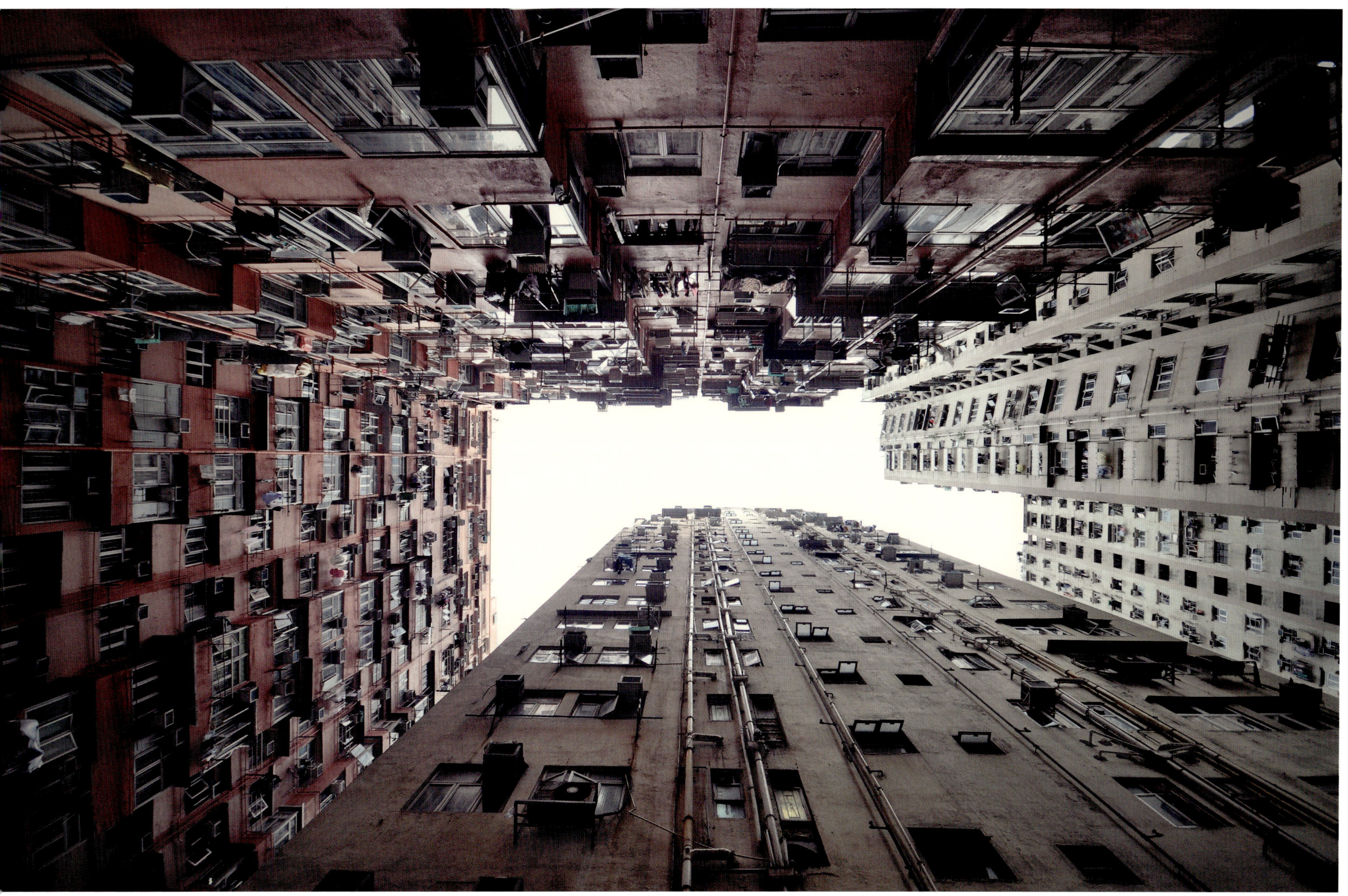

圍城

Besieger

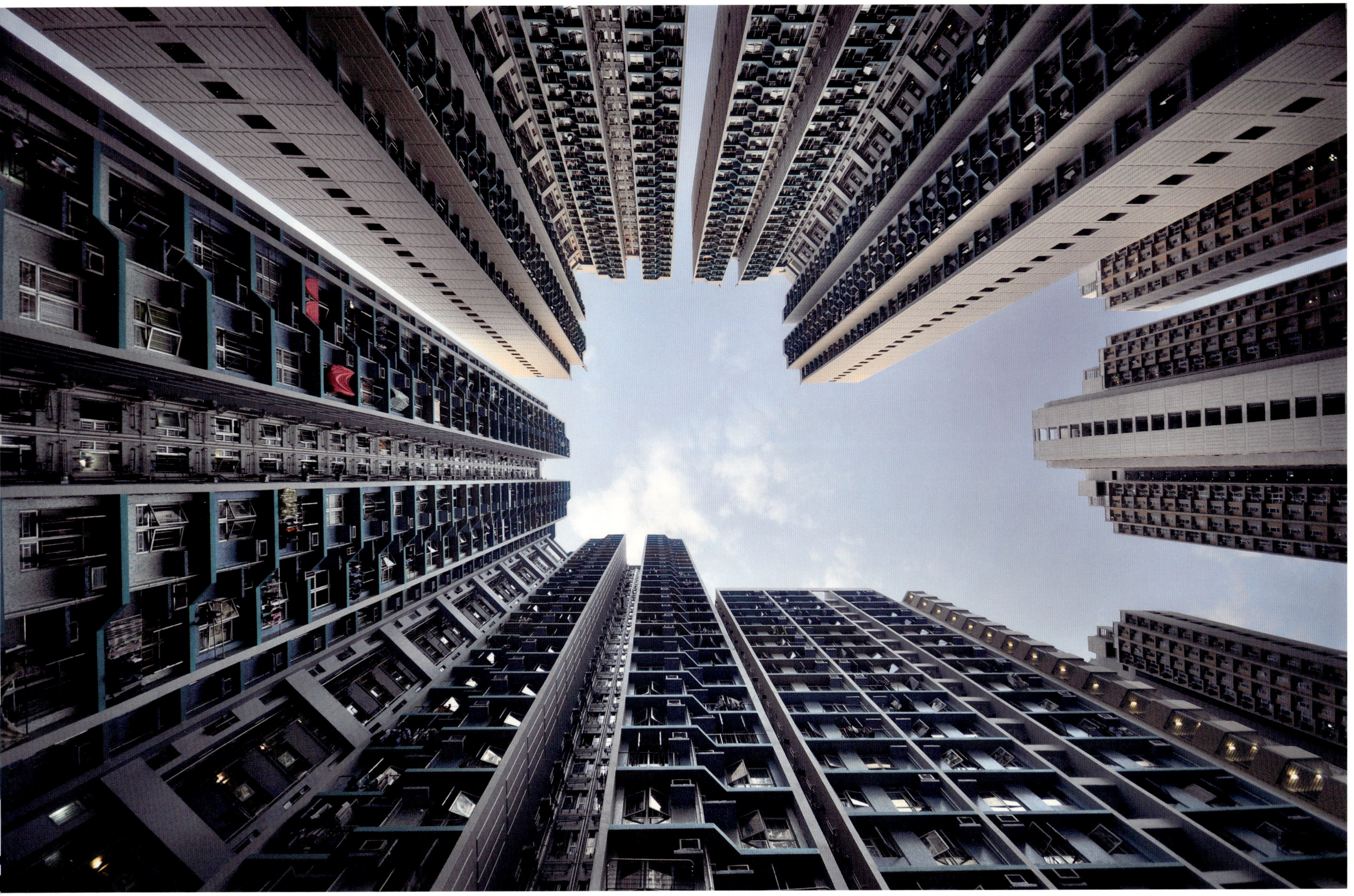

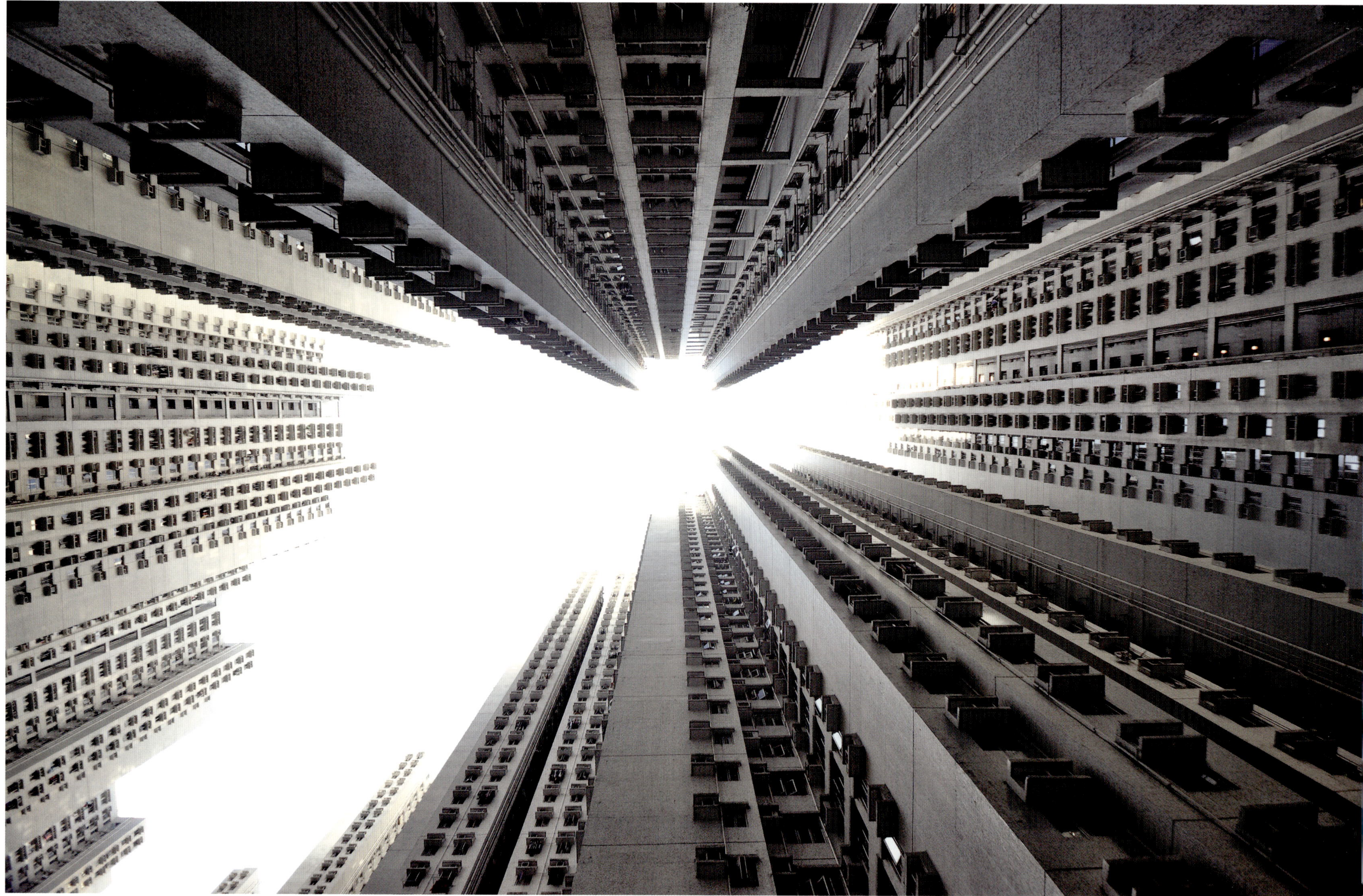

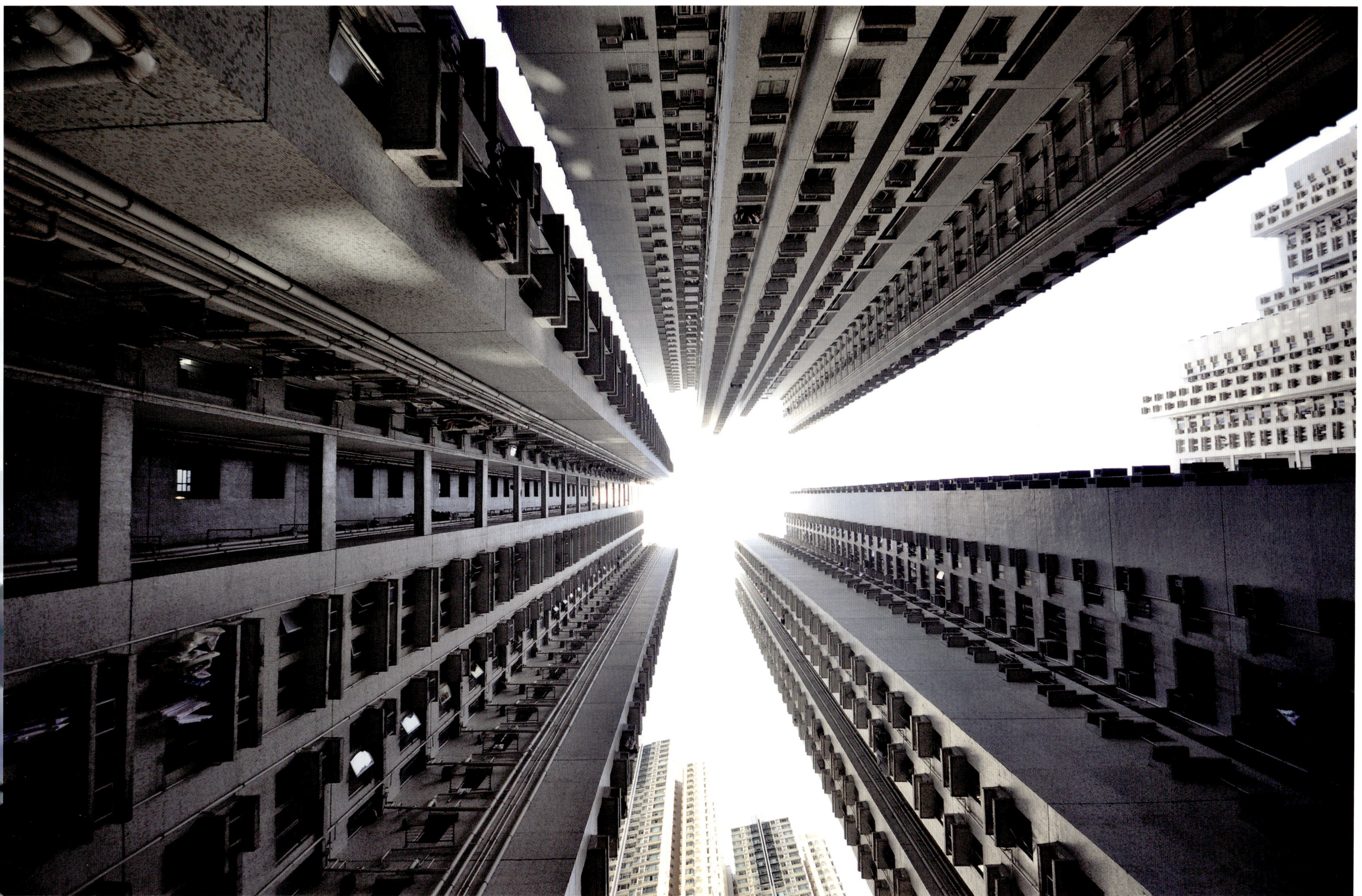

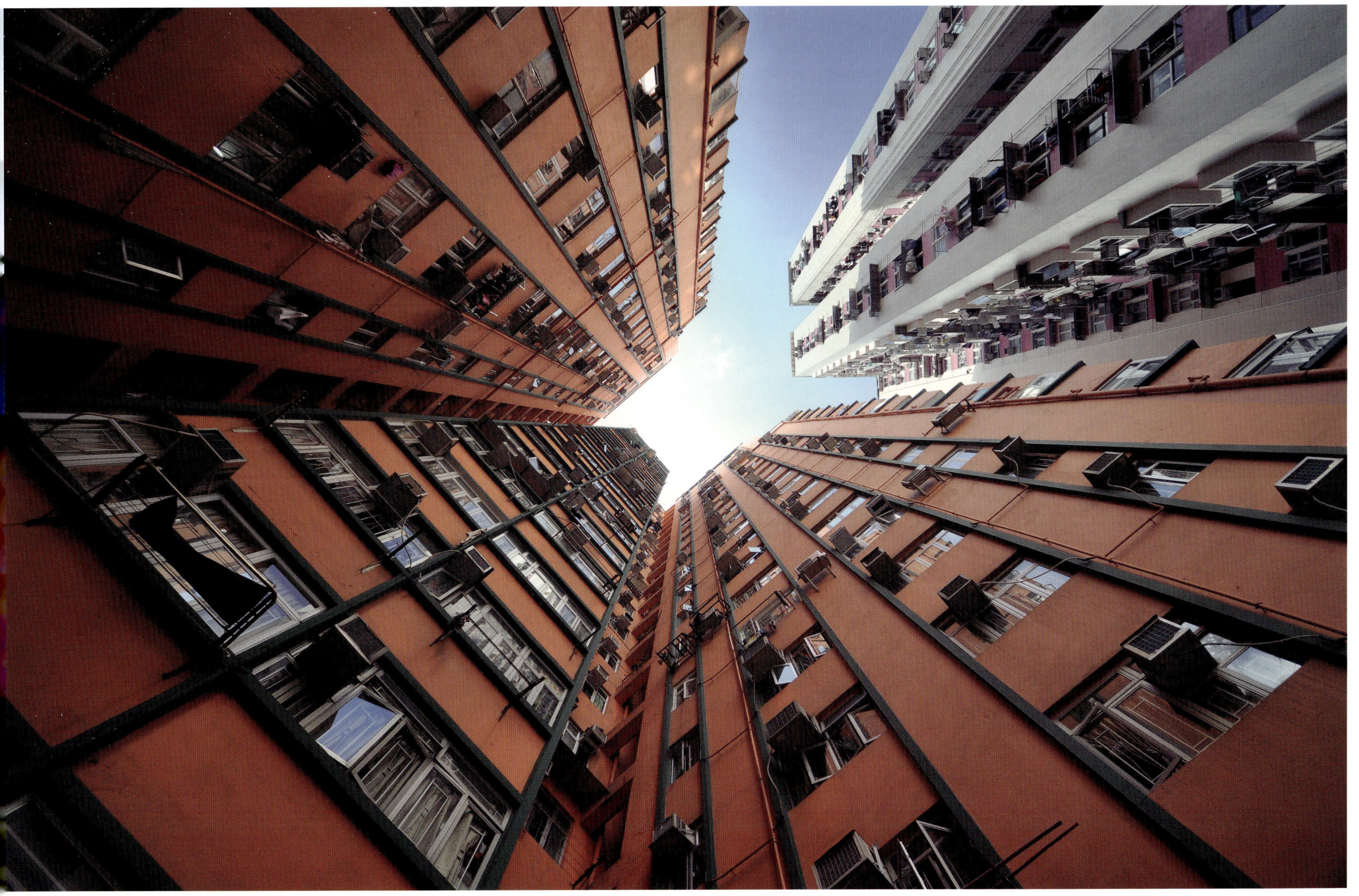

集聚

Convergence

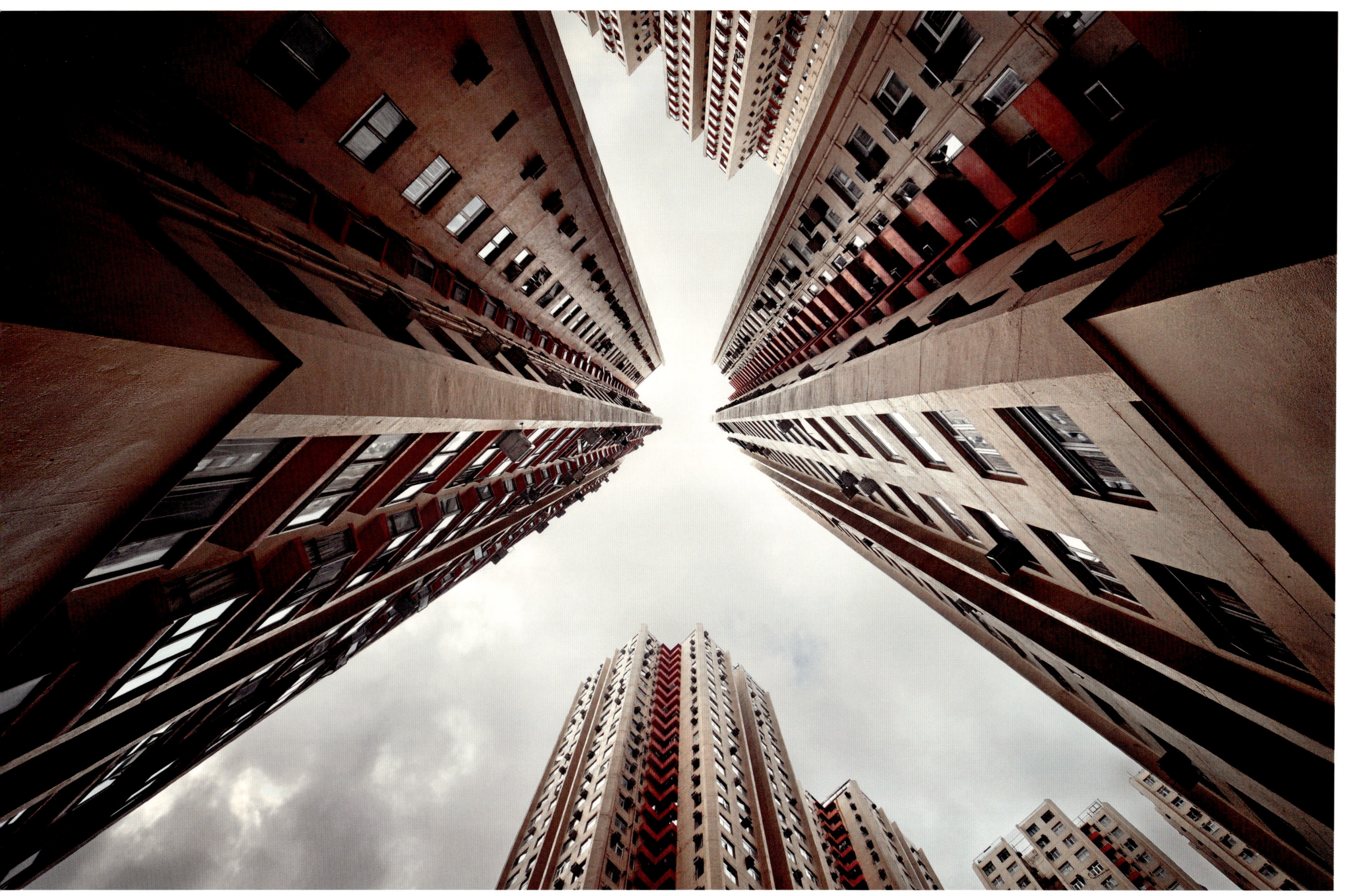

對稱
Symmetry

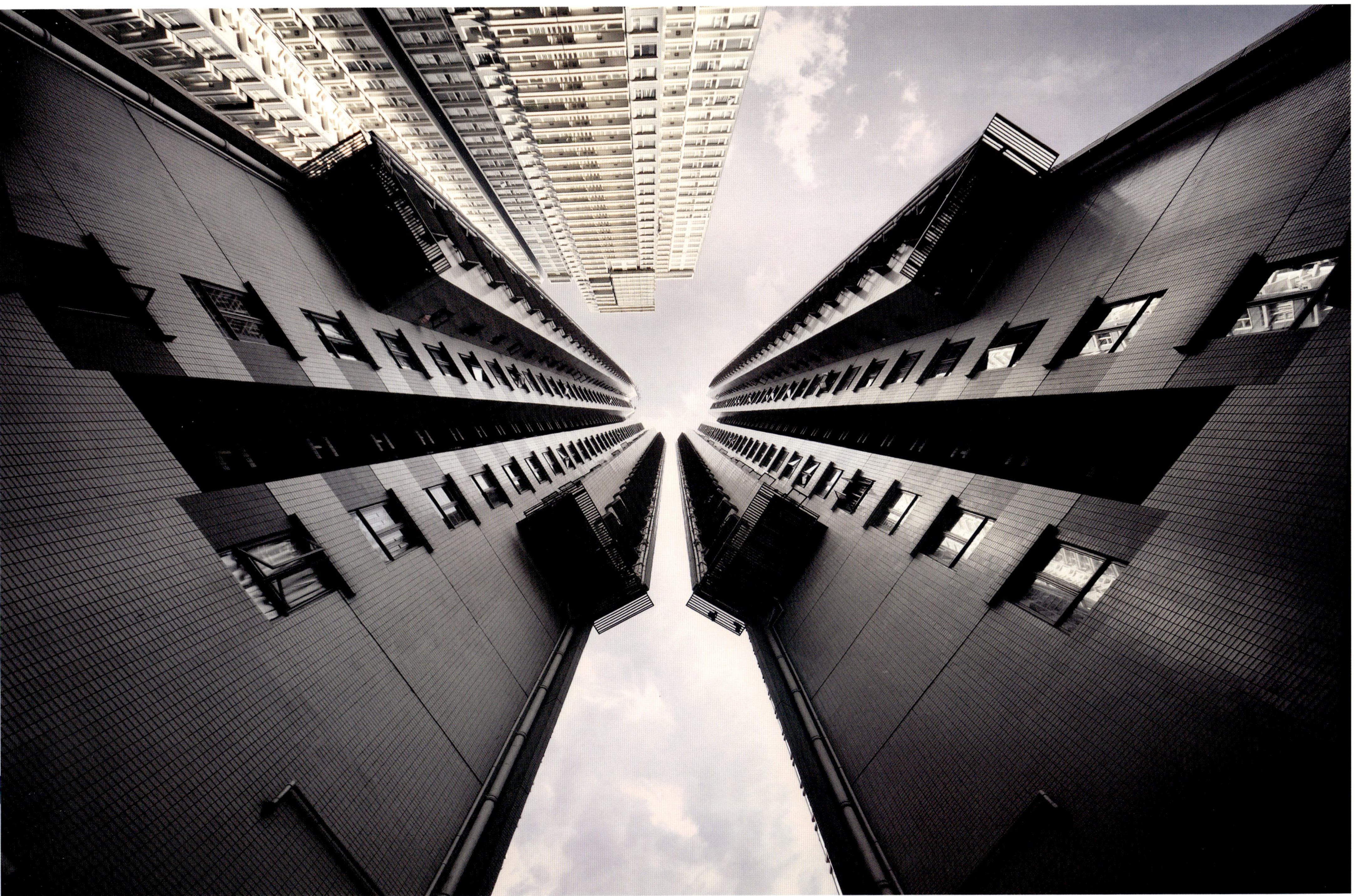

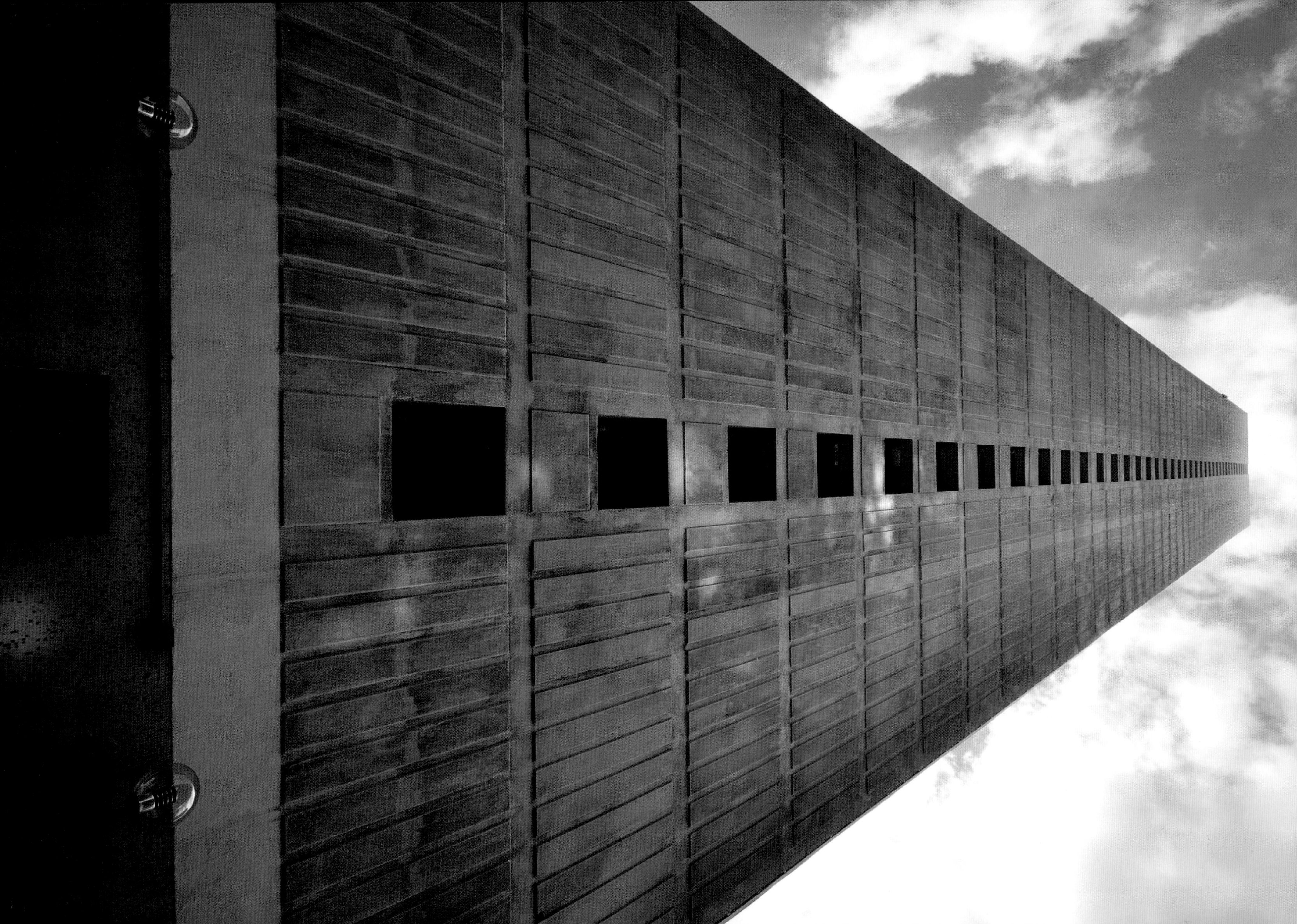

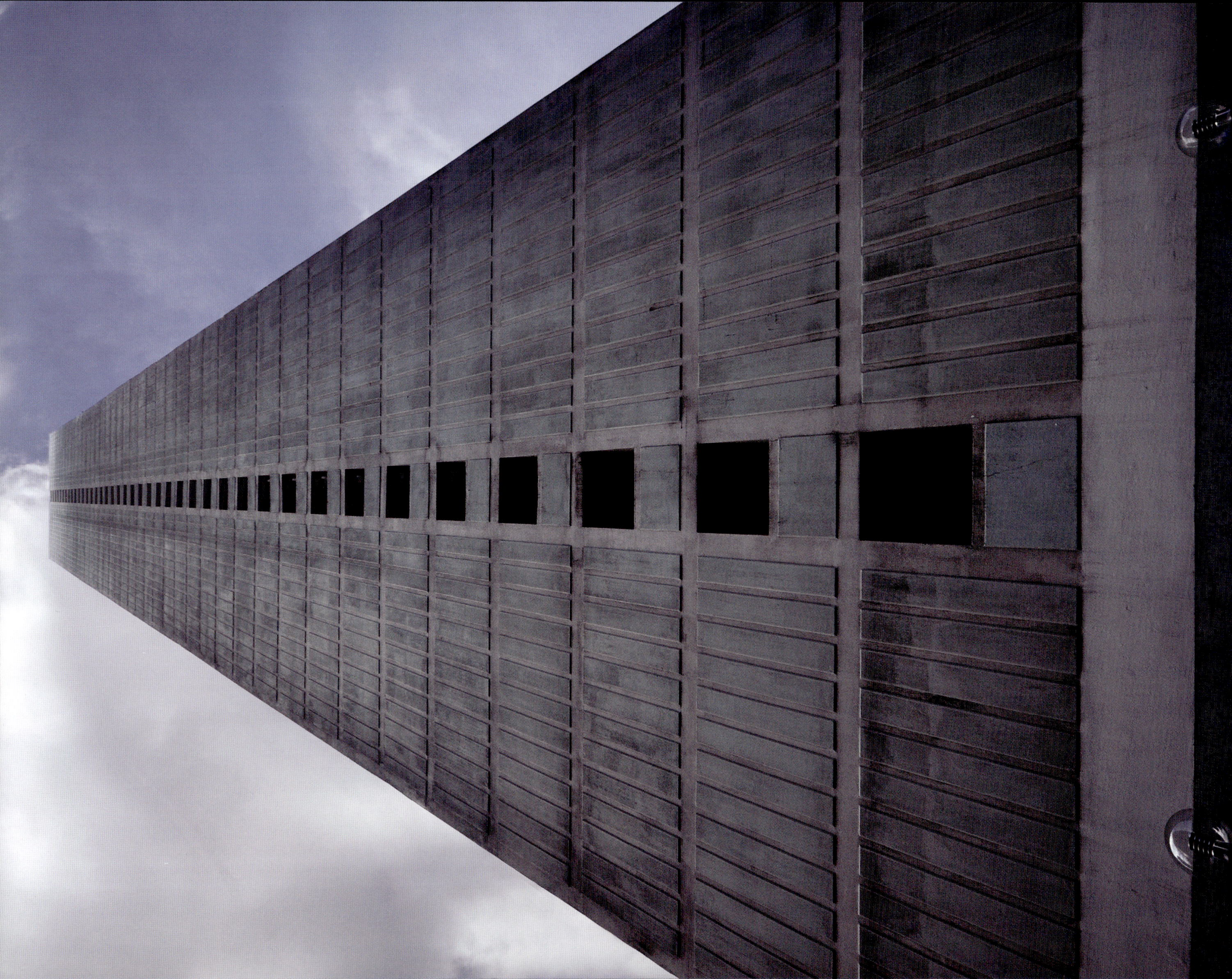

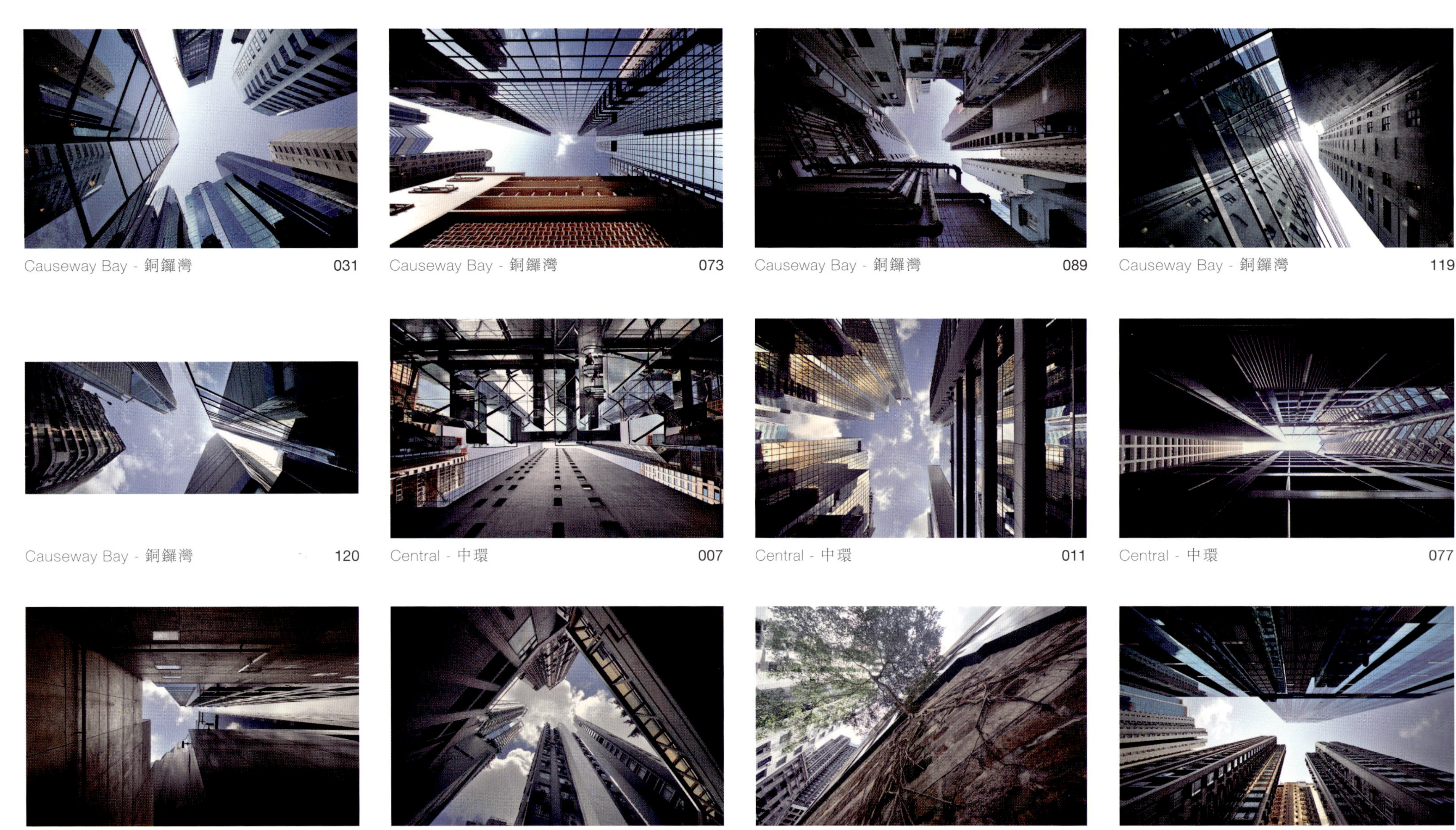

Causeway Bay - 銅鑼灣 031

Causeway Bay - 銅鑼灣 073

Causeway Bay - 銅鑼灣 089

Causeway Bay - 銅鑼灣 119

Causeway Bay - 銅鑼灣 120

Central - 中環 007

Central - 中環 011

Central - 中環 077

Central - 中環 079

Mid-Levels - 半山區 081

Mid-Levels - 半山區 093

North Point - 北角 009

Hong Kong Island / 香港島

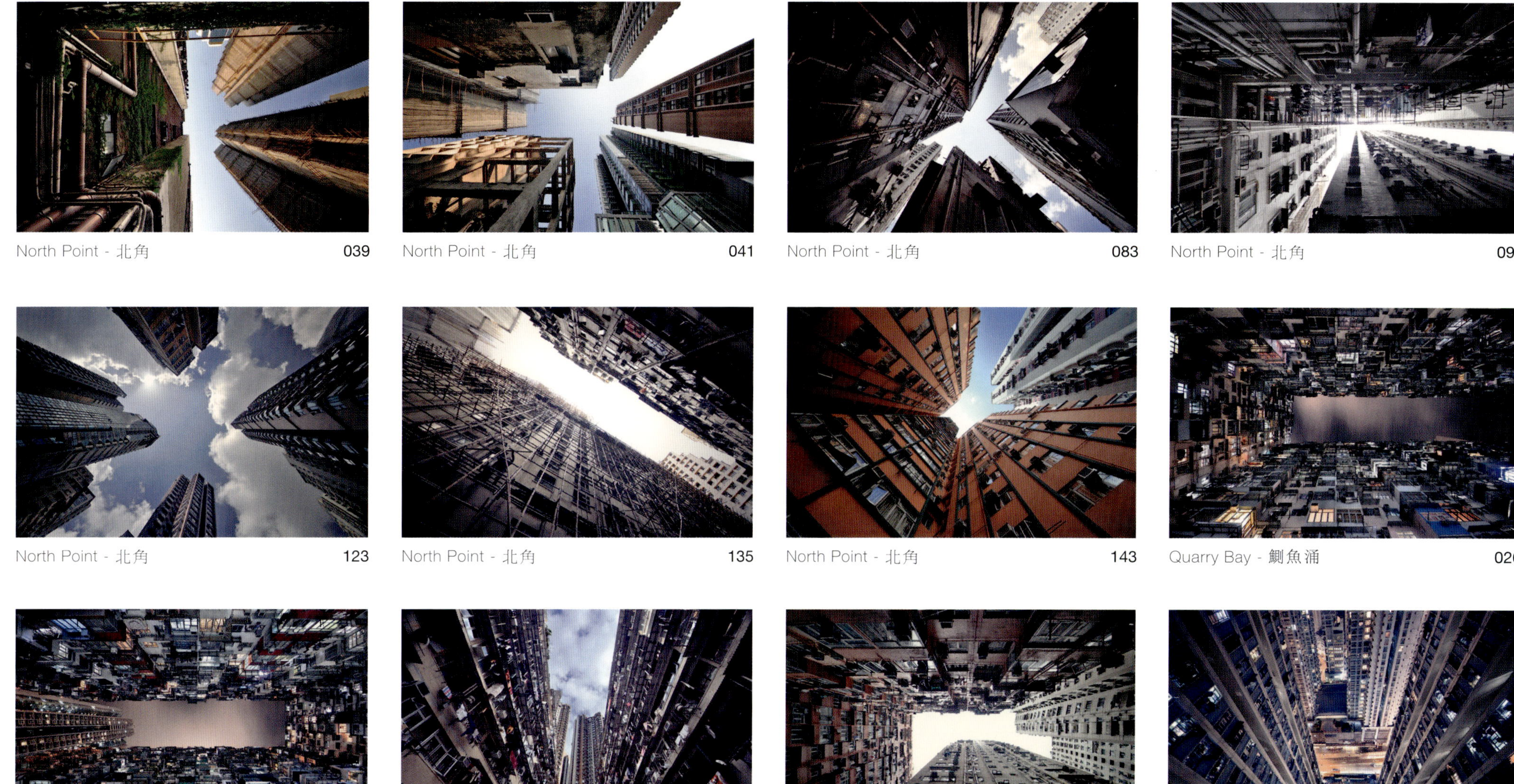

North Point - 北角 039

North Point - 北角 041

North Point - 北角 083

North Point - 北角 097

North Point - 北角 123

North Point - 北角 135

North Point - 北角 143

Quarry Bay - 鰂魚涌 026

Quarry Bay - 鰂魚涌 027

Quarry Bay - 鰂魚涌 107

Quarry Bay - 鰂魚涌 137

Sai Wan Ho - 西灣河 110

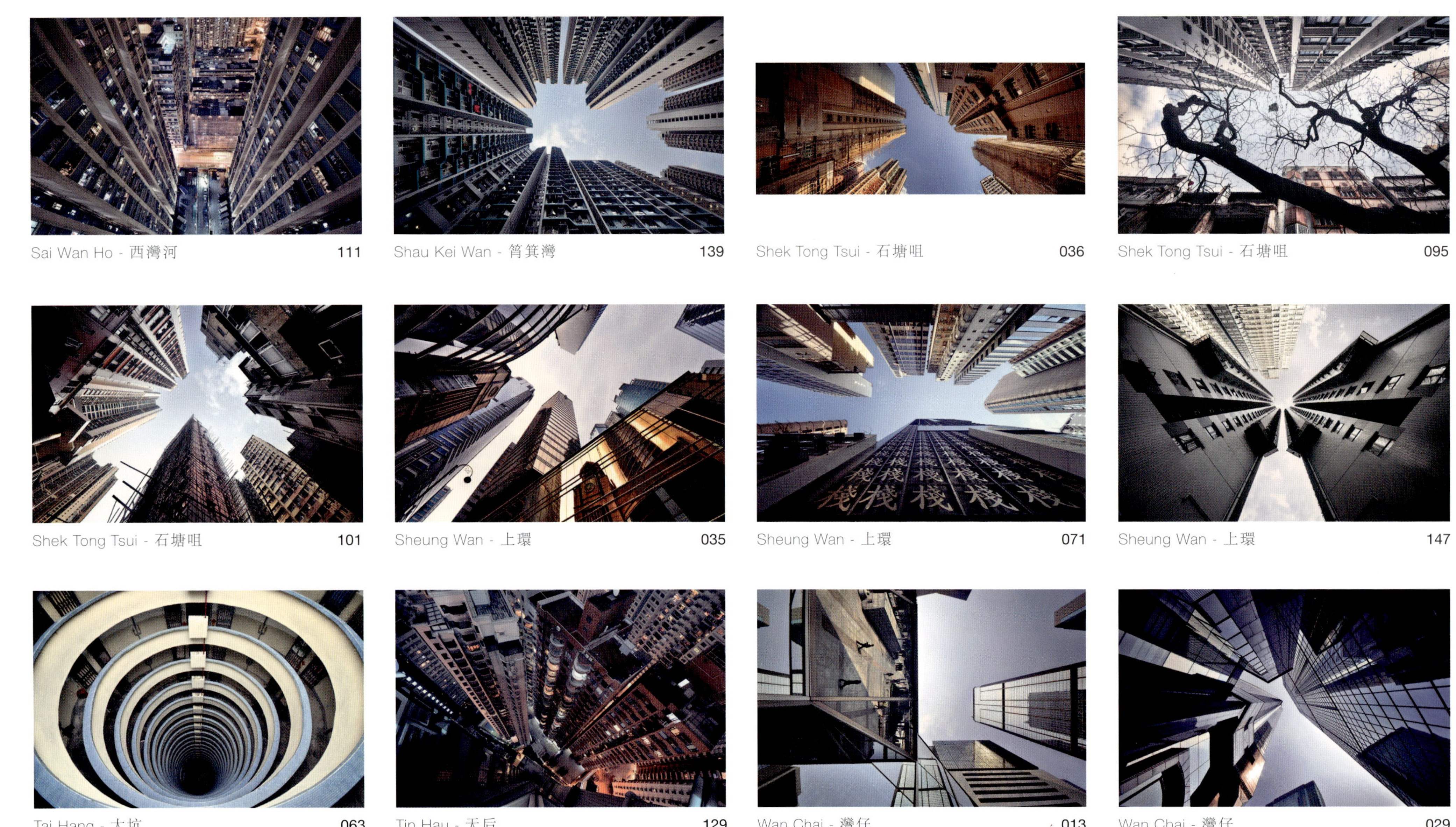

Sai Wan Ho - 西灣河 111

Shau Kei Wan - 筲箕灣 139

Shek Tong Tsui - 石塘咀 036

Shek Tong Tsui - 石塘咀 095

Shek Tong Tsui - 石塘咀 101

Sheung Wan - 上環 035

Sheung Wan - 上環 071

Sheung Wan - 上環 147

Tai Hang - 大坑 063

Tin Hau - 天后 129

Wan Chai - 灣仔 013

Wan Chai - 灣仔 029

Hong Kong Island / 香港島

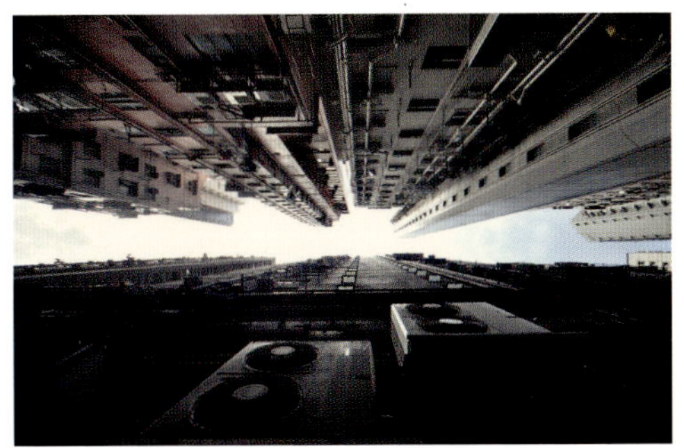

Wan Chai - 灣仔 045

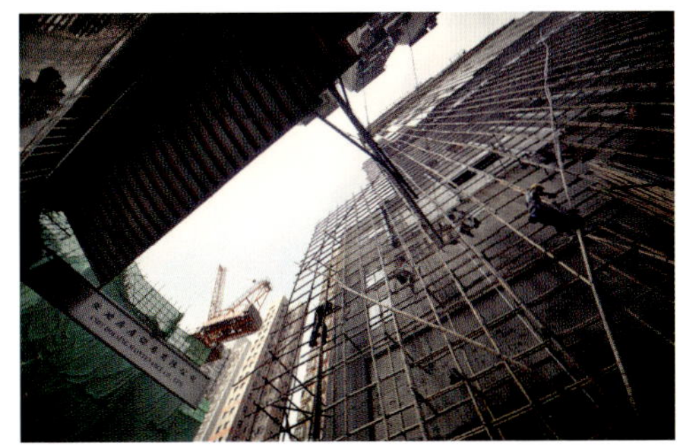

Wan Chai - 灣仔 099

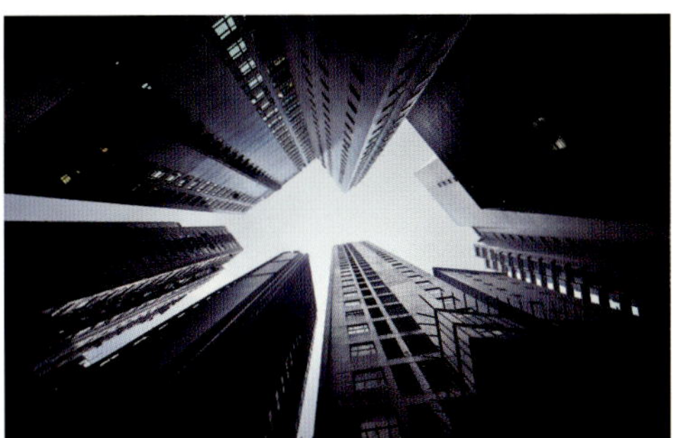

Wan Chai - 灣仔 115

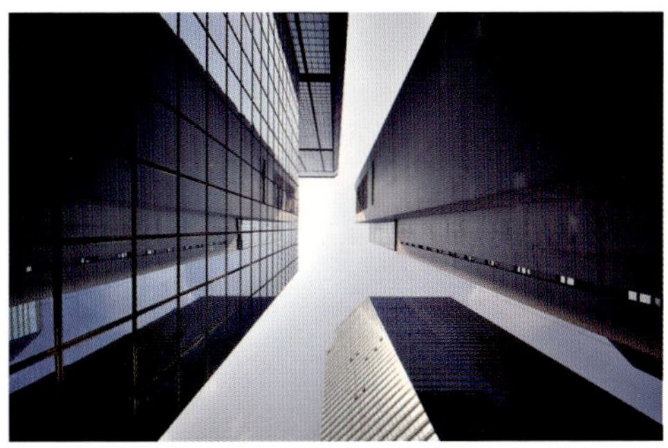

Wan Chai - 灣仔 117

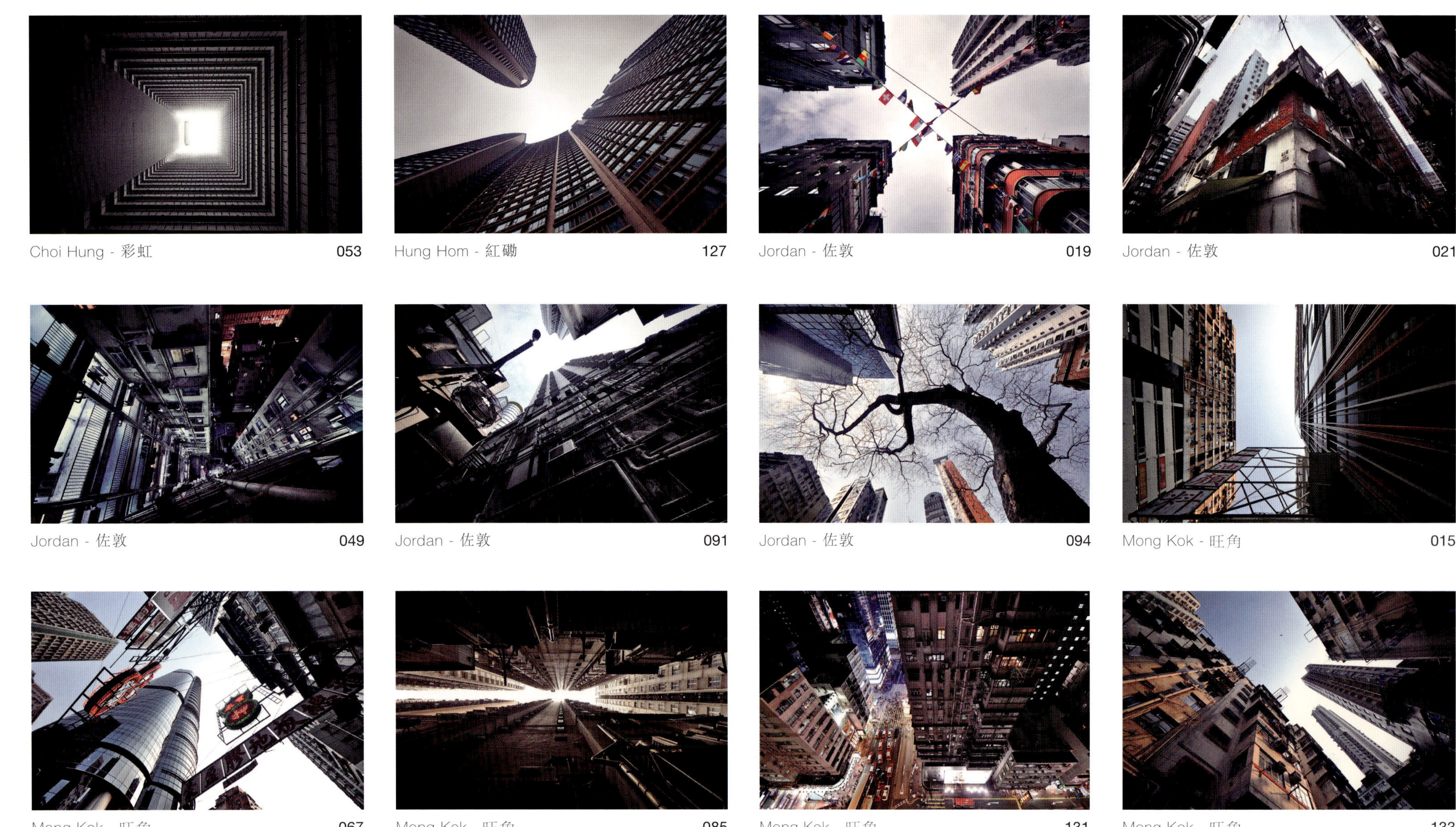

Kowloon / 九龍

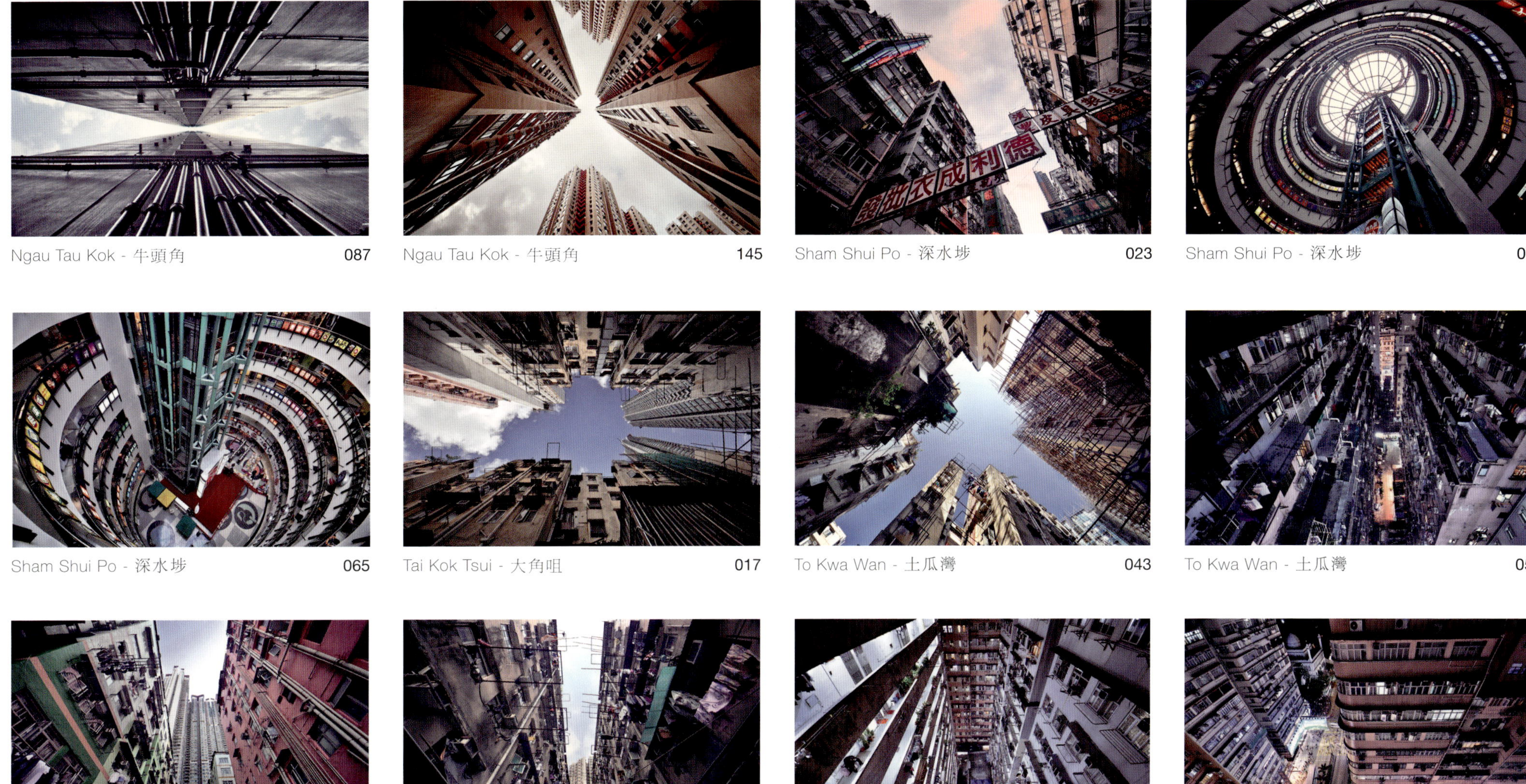

Ngau Tau Kok - 牛頭角 087

Ngau Tau Kok - 牛頭角 145

Sham Shui Po - 深水埗 023

Sham Shui Po - 深水埗 064

Sham Shui Po - 深水埗 065

Tai Kok Tsui - 大角咀 017

To Kwa Wan - 土瓜灣 043

To Kwa Wan - 土瓜灣 051

To Kwa Wan - 土瓜灣 103

To Kwa Wan - 土瓜灣 105

To Kwa Wan - 土瓜灣 109

Tsim Sha Tsui - 尖沙咀 025

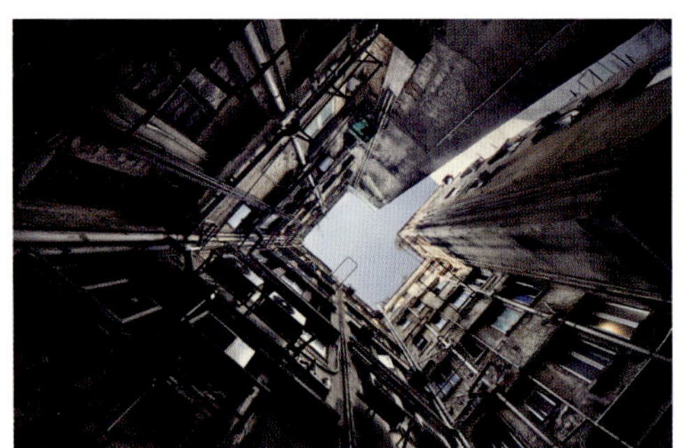

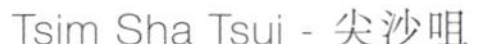

Tsim Sha Tsui - 尖沙咀 047

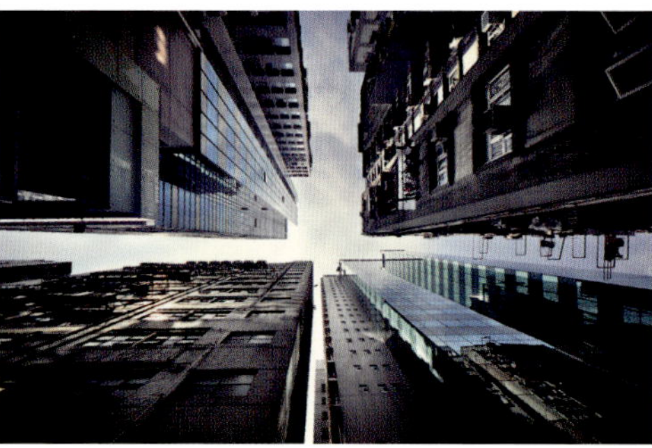

Tsim Sha Tsui - 尖沙咀 069

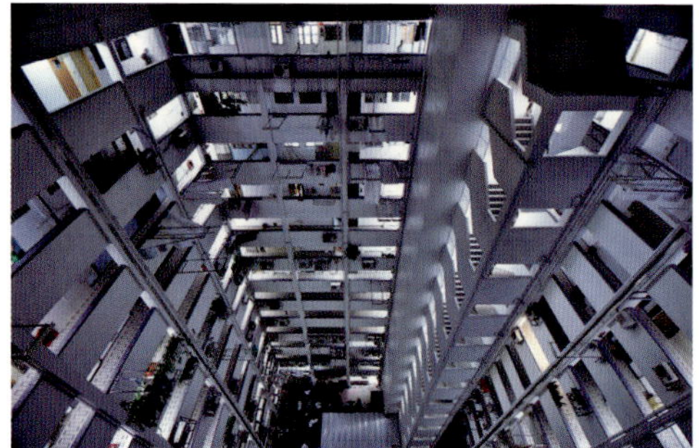

Tsim Sha Tsui - 尖沙咀 113

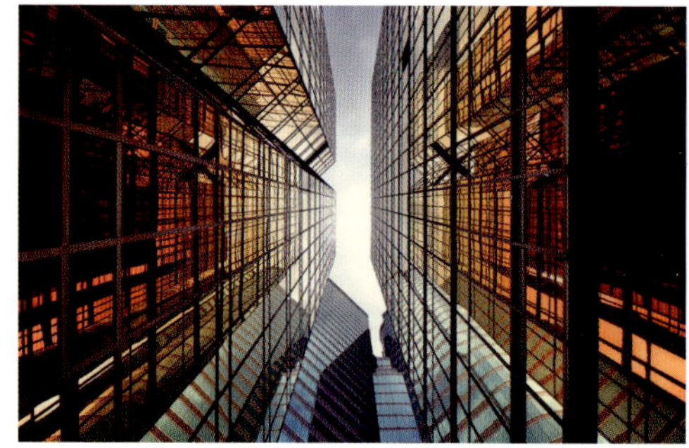

Tsim Sha Tsui West - 尖沙咀西 032

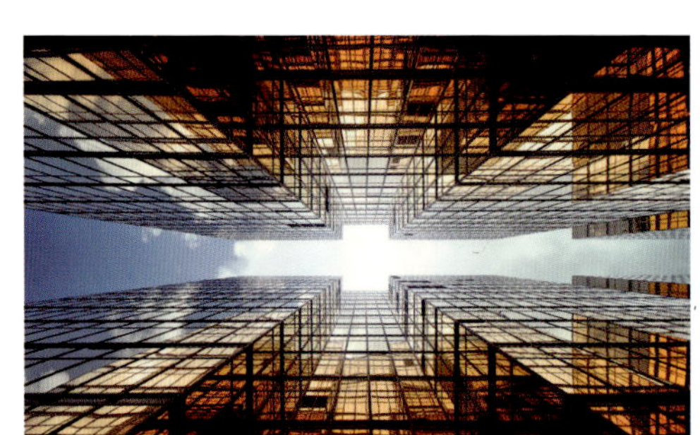

Tsim Sha Tsui West - 尖沙咀西 033

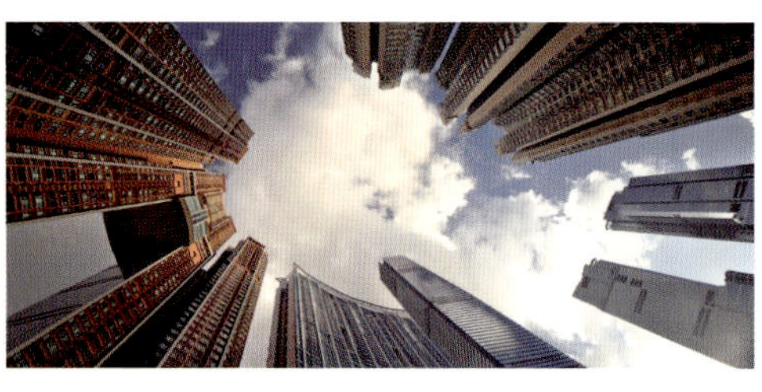

Tsim Sha Tsui West - 尖沙咀西 124

Kowloon / 九龍

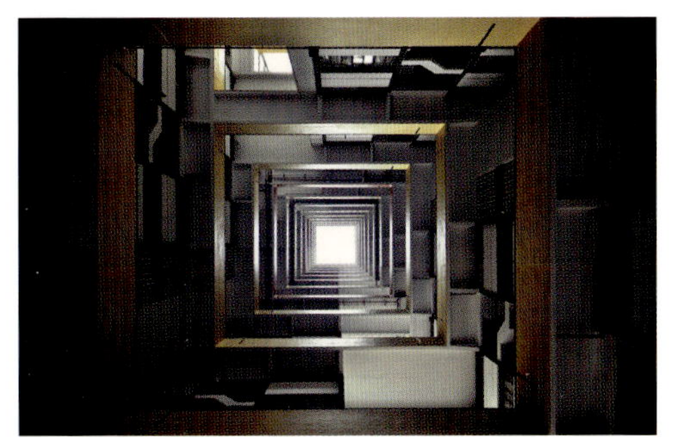

Lai King - 荔景 061

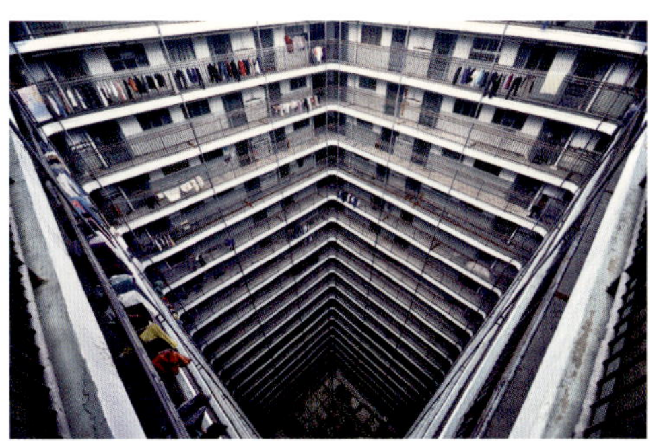
Lai King - 荔景 074

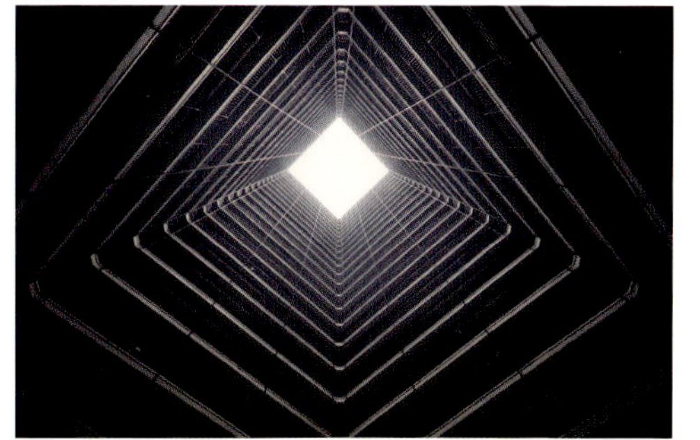
Lai King - 荔景 075

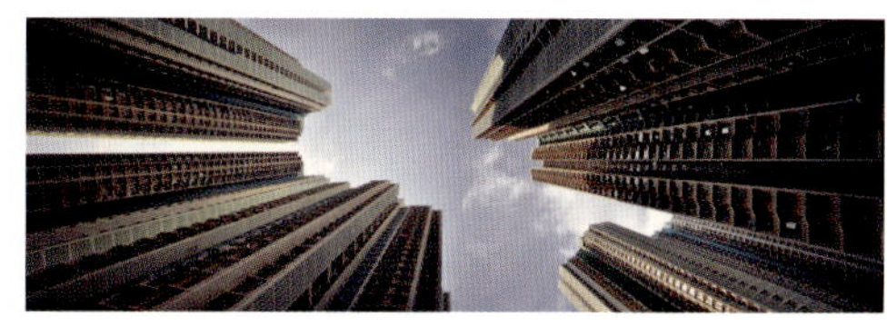
Tin Shui Wai - 天水圍 002

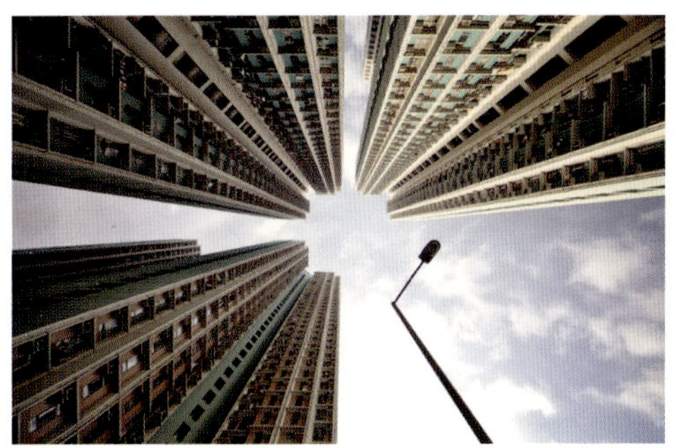
Tin Shui Wai - 天水圍 059

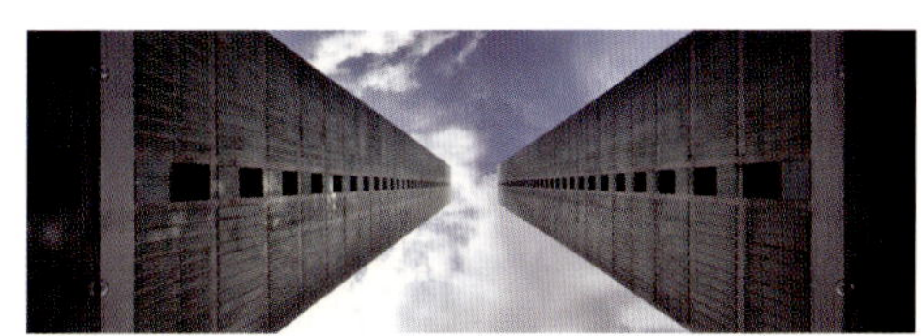
Tin Shui Wai - 天水圍 148

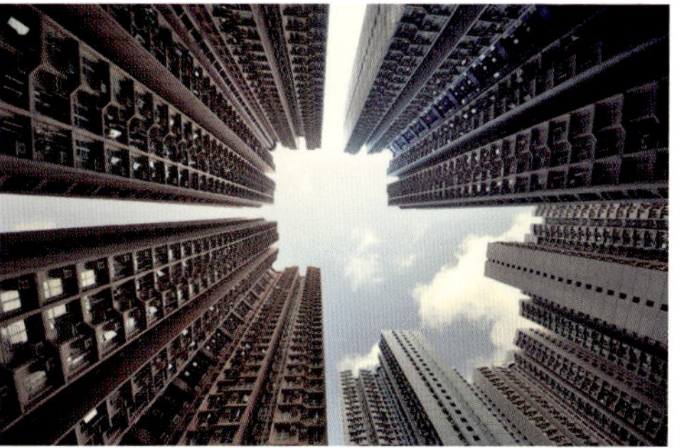
Tseung Kwan O - 將軍澳 055

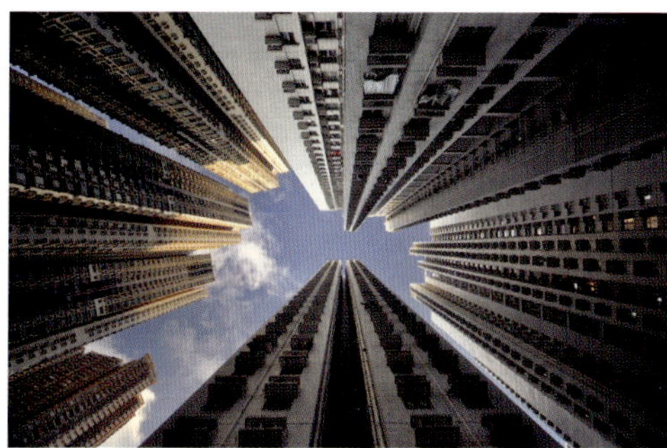
Tseung Kwan O - 將軍澳 057

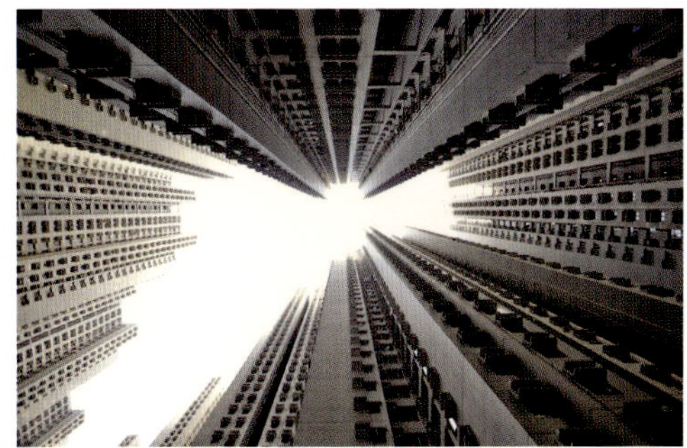
Tseung Kwan O - 將軍澳 140

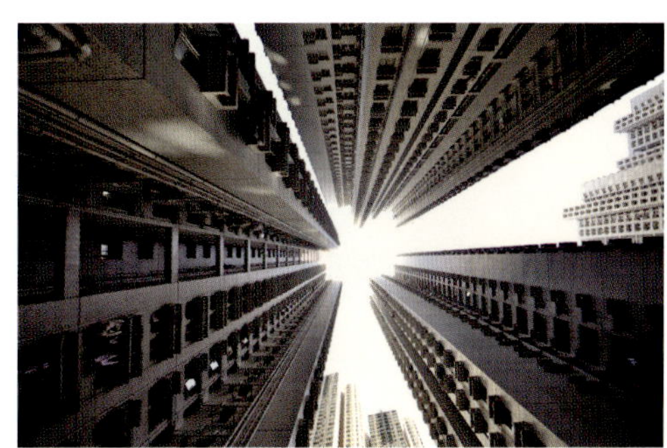
Tseung Kwan O - 將軍澳 141

New Territories / 新界

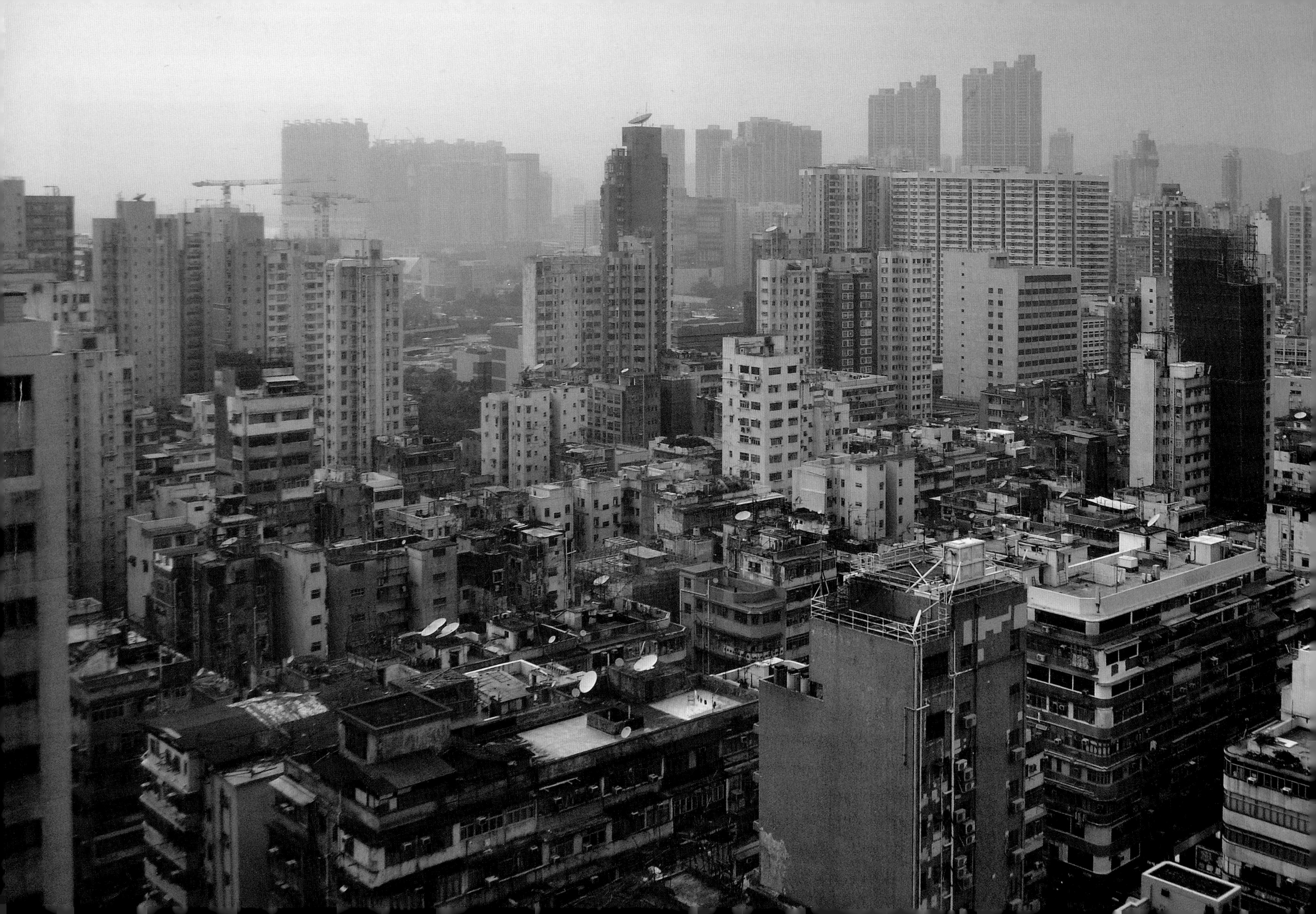